PRAISE FOR ABBOT VONIER'S
A Key to the Doctrine of the Eucharist

"This is a beautiful book—one of the great treasures of the Catholic renewal of the last century."
— CHRISTOPH CARDINAL SCHÖNBORN

"One could wish most earnestly that every Catholic—and every Protestant for that matter—would read Abbot Vonier's book. Both the mystery and the richness of the Eucharist are here: but the book is splendidly readable—no small achievement."
— THOMAS HOWARD, author, *Evangelical Is Not Enough*

"Stephen Langton, the 13th-century Archbishop of Canterbury, famously said, 'If you wish to learn, five things are necessary: purity of life, simplicity of heart, an attentive mind, a humble disposition, and a gentle spirit.'
"Abbot Vonier's book on the Eucharist exemplifies the beauty and radiance of all five of these virtues. Not since St. Thomas Aquinas's treatment of this sacrament in the *Tertia Pars* of his *Summa Theologiae* has there been a more lucid and serene presentation of the Catholic understanding of the Eucharist than this book. It should be required reading in every course in sacramental theology in every Catholic seminary and college in the nation."
— EDWARD T. OAKES, S.J., Chester & Margaret Paluch Professor of Theology, University of St. Mary of the Lake/Mundelein Seminary

"Abbot Vonier's book is characterized by sparkling clarity of thought. It isn't terribly difficult to read, but it goes slowly because each chapter is a stunning revelation."
— STEVEN RIDDLE, *Flos Carmeli* weblog

"*A Key to the Doctrine of the Eucharist* is like a breath of fresh air. Thoroughly imbued with the spirit and thought of St. Thomas, I find myself reading each chapter twice, in some cases just to savor the fresh way the author explains the topic, and in other cases to see what I missed."

— Fr. Jeffrey Keyes, c.pp.s., *The New Gasparian* weblog
Pastor of St. Edward Parish, Newark, California

"*A Key to the Doctrine of the Eucharist* is one of the few classics in Catholic theology composed in English. Correcting an excessive split between the sacrifice of the Mass and the sacrament of the Eucharist, Vonier found a better theory in Thomas Aquinas, that of 'sacramental sacrifice.' His proposal, controversial in his own day, is in harmony with the recent teaching of the Magisterium and is widely accepted by theologians of our time. This book, remarkable for its balance, depth, and accessibility, should never be out of print."

— Avery Cardinal Dulles, s.j.

"A challenging but worthwhile book. Abbot Vonier explains the Catholic doctrine of the Real Presence with clarity and precision by focusing on the sacramental element in the Eucharist. Chapters 20, 21 and 22 are especially compelling, and could stand alone as independent essays."

— Oswald Sobrino, *Catholic Analysis* weblog

"Highly recommended. There is much here to nourish you intellectually, and also to nourish your contemplative prayer life in reflecting on the great gift that God has given us in the Eucharist."

— Jeff Miller, *The Curt Jester* weblog

"An excellent book. Abbot Vonier's writing is profound enough to yield a deeper meaning each time it is pondered."

— Tom Kreitzberg, *Disputations* weblog

*A Key to the Doctrine
of the Eucharist*

BOOKS BY

Abbot Vonier

A Key
to the
Doctrine
of the
Eucharist

Abbot Vonier

ZACCHEUS PRESS
Bethesda

Nihil Obstat: Thomas McLaughlin, S.T.D.
             Deputy Censor

Imprimatur: Edm. Can. Surmont
             Vicar General, Westminster
             February 5, 1925

Library of Congress Cataloging-in-Publication Data
Vonier, Anscar, 1875-1938.
   A key to the doctrine of the Eucharist / by Abbot Vonier.
      p. cm.
Includes index.
   ISBN 0-9725981-0-3 (pbk. : alk. paper)
   1. Lord's Supper—Catholic Church. I. Title.
   BX2215.3 .V66 2003
   234'.163—dc21
                                                    2003008678

10 9 8 7 6 5 4

To learn more about Abbot Vonier, please visit our webpage:

www.zaccheuspress.com

Contents

Preface

I am not a professional theologian, but a philosopher; but I read more theology than philosophy, and I have seldom read such a convincing, clear, and comprehensive study in Eucharistic theology as *A Key to the Doctrine of the Eucharist*.

Its theological depth comes largely from its fidelity to, and its power to illuminate, the Church's sacred Tradition concerning the Eucharist, and to show very clearly the profundity and reasonableness of the writings of Saint Thomas Aquinas and of the Council of Trent, and how they are rooted in Scripture and the earliest Fathers of the Church. Abbot Vonier makes them intelligible through a philosophy and a literary style that is utterly lucid, penetrating, and humble—rather like that of Saint Thomas himself. Although I had not been familiar with his work, having now read *Key*—a jewel of a book—I look forward to discovering more of Abbot Vonier's work as Zaccheus Press continues its project of reissuing it.

The most stunning effect this book had on me was the realization of the shallow and ephemeral nature of most current theology, by comparison. We don't seem to produce theological thinkers like this anymore. Perhaps this book will begin to remedy that lack, by instructing apprentices and stimulating us to imitation. We dwarfs had better start standing on the shoulders of giants like this, as Father Vonier himself clearly has done.

PETER KREEFT

Introduction

Anscar Vonier was the most gifted dogmatic theologian writing—and preaching—in England during the inter-War years. By an unexpected blessing, the English Catholic Church had in its midst a German monk of outstanding competence and spiritual nobility. Born on November 11, 1875, Vonier had left his native Wuerttemberg (still a kingdom in 1888, though within the German Empire) so as to enter a French abbey: La Pierre-qui-Vire in the *plateau du Morvan*, a bleak and windswept corner of Burgundy. In fortuitous political circumstances he fetched up instead in the valley of the Dart, where that river sweeps down from Dartmoor to the open sea.

In one of the recurring Church-State crises which punctuated the history of the Third French Republic, the monks of Le Pierre-qui-Vire had abandoned France for (as was thought) a temporary exile in Britain. So it was Dom Vonier found himself a member of a new monastic foundation—or, rather, *re*-foundation, as the history of Buckfast goes back to the Anglo-Saxon period. This was by no means the end of squalls. As a young priest accompanying his abbot on canonical visitation to Argentina, he endured, off the Spanish coast, the shipwreck of the liner *Sirio* which took his companion's life on August 4, 1906. Anscar Vonier was elected abbot in his place at the extraordinarily early age of 31.

As his fame grew, it became impossible *not* to think of him as *Abbot* Vonier. He who had been the youngest reigning abbot in the Benedictine federation would remain in office until his death on December 26, 1938. To the ordinary English Catholic, he was best known as the rebuilder of Buckfast, which is still the only pre-Reformation monastic house in England to be reconstructed for its original purpose, with a great church worthy of the medieval abbeys. To *cognoscenti* of sermons on major Church occasions, Abbot Vonier belonged to a charmed circle of great preachers—Martindale, Jarrett, McNabb, Goodier, Knox—of the 1920s and 30s. That is eloquent of his mastery of what was in point of fact his third language. Endowed with a powerful charism of preaching, he made the English tongue a vigorous instrument for the exposition of Catholic truth. To Catholic readers, that is not least apparent in the prose works where he gave his theological vision, in equal share biblical and Thomistic, a lasting expression. In the priority he gave, within the round of monastic life, to the production of solid works of doctrinal theology for the use of both clergy and laity, he had—dare one say it!—a Dominican approach to the Benedictine way. Writing came next to the *Opus Dei*, the celebration of the liturgy, not least because it drew life from the liturgy, overflowed from it.

First published in 1925, *A Key to the Doctrine of the Eucharist* was evidently written as a Thomist rejoinder to the much-acclaimed and influential *Mysterium Fidei*, a study of the Mass by the French Jesuit Maurice de la Taille (Paris, 1921). Under the heading "A New Theory of the Eucharistic Sacrifice," the Dominican Vincent McNabb, writing in *Blackfriars* for September 1924, had already criticized one major feature in de la Taille's work. De la Taille had argued that the Last Supper constituted the priestly oblation by Christ of the flesh that, by bloody slaughter, was sacrificed on the Cross. This implies that, considered as the sacrifice of our redemption, Calvary was incomplete without the foregoing Supper and what took place there. It also implies that the first Mass, which the Lord Himself celebrated in the Upper Room, is more truly the opening phase of the Sacrifice of Christ than it is the sacramental presentation of that Sacrifice.

Discreetly, without ever mentioning de la Taille by name, Abbot Vonier seconds McNabb's criticism (whether by chance or through a conscious process I do not know). But his real target (if the phrase may be used of so thoroughly positive a book as the *Key*) is not de la Taille, the individual writer, so much as the entire school of thought which, particularly in France, sought to describe the Eucharistic sacrifice in terms drawn elsewhere than from sacramental theology.

Whether by looking to other portions of Christian dogmatics, especially Christology, or by attempting to find general definitions of sacrifice that would suit the case, such authors, in Vonier's view, missed the essential point. The Holy Eucharist is first and foremost the Holy Sacrifice not because it is something different from a mere sacrament but because it is, precisely as taught by Saint Thomas, *the sacrament of the Sacrifice of Christ*.

Vonier believed Saint Thomas's approach to be the right one because it gives the clearest account of all the realities involved in their inter-relation. Indeed, it is their ability to inter-relate the various doctrines of the faith, and the circumambient realities with which they deal, that makes both Aquinas and Vonier theologians worth following. But Vonier does not simply re-peat Thomas's texts. Like all good disciples he is a thoughtful interpreter and not merely an unreflective codifier. So the eucharistic theologian Thomas Aquinas who emerges from *Key* is significantly different from any other. Above all, he is from first to last a theologian of the sign: what, in the early twenty-first century would be called a "semiotic" theologian. The world of natural reality and the sign-world of sacramental reality are two different worlds, and yet, in the case of the Eucharistic sacrifice, they yield up to us the same content. The sacrifice of the Mass is the expression in sign of all that our great high priest in his once-for-all offering on the Cross underwent, did, and was. Calvary and the Mass are the self-same reality, in two utterly different modes.

A Key to the Doctrine of the Eucharist provides the patient reader (this is no tract to be devoured in half-an-hour!) with a complete theology of the Holy Eucharist. This is so even if, as the author admits, the section on Holy Communion is too short. It is still true, even if, as the present writer would claim, Vonier's rejection of the notion of the *sacrificium coeleste*—any sense in which the exalted crucified Lord, now in heaven, remains in the posture of sacrifice before his Father—is too hastily made.

But the value of this book to the Catholic reader in the post-Conciliar period will not only be to give him or her an idea of how rigorous—and yet religiously exhilarating—the best Catholic theology can be. It will also be to recall them to the conviction of the Church of all ages that the Mass is not primarily assembly or common meal, not primarily Holy Communion or anticipation of the heavenly Banquet. It is primarily *the Church's sacrifice*, the Christian Oblation. It is on the identity of the Holy Eucharist with Christ's glorious Passion, offered and accepted, that all the fruits of the Eucharist depend, and all the other values and aspects liturgists see in Eucharistic celebration turn.

AIDAN NICHOLS, O.P.

Blackfriars, Cambridge
Memorial Day of Saints Basil and Gregory, 2003

A Key to the Doctrine
of the Eucharist

1

Faith

The Catholic doctrine of the Eucharist is a particular instance of the more universal question of the mode of our union with Christ. We take for granted the Incarnation and the Atonement on the Cross; we take for granted that the Son of God through His death has redeemed mankind in general and has satisfied for sin; we know that in Christ there is plentiful redemption; such things are for us unchallengeable and universal articles of belief which may be called God's side of the matter, that aspect of truth which is turned heavenward.

But the universal truths thus enunciated leave untouched that other problem of our own individual share in the treasures of redemption—how do individual men come into contact with that great Christ who is our Redemption personified? There is evidently in the Christian doctrine of redemption an element so absolute that it stands by itself, quite independent of man's benefit therefrom. Before it is at all possible to think of man's enrichment through the grace of Christ's redemption we have to assume that much greater result of Christ's sacrifice on the Cross which is aptly expressed in the term "Atonement," by which is meant, not directly the benefit of man, but the benefit of God: that full restoration of what had been taken from God through man's sin, His honor and glory. Christ's act on the Cross has given back to the Father all that was ever taken away from Him by man, and the divine rights have been fully restored.

It is not an absurd hypothesis to think of Christ's great act of atonement as having an exclusively divine side—that is to say, Christ could have died on the Cross with the exclusive purpose of giving back to the Father all the glory which He had lost through man's transgression, without the human race being in any way the better for it. But this is merely an hypothesis, though a perfectly rational one. Actually Catholic doctrine says that Christ's sacrifice, besides being an atonement, was also a redemption—in other words, a buying back into spiritual liberty of the human race which had become the slave of evil. But even this aspect of Christ's divine act, though a perfectly human one, is still too universal; salvation is primarily for mankind as a species; the entry of the individual into the redemptive plan remains to be effected.

The urgent problem is, how am I to be linked up effectively with that great mystery of Christ's death? When shall I know that Christ is not only the Redeemer, but also *my* Redeemer? Mere membership with the human race does not link me up with Christ, though it be true that Christ died for the whole race. This membership is indeed a condition, *sine qua non*, of my becoming one day a member of Christ; but a member of Christ I shall not become unless some new realities be brought into play. These new realities which are the link between me and Christ are faith and the sacraments.

"The power of Christ's passion," says Saint Thomas, "is linked up with us through faith and through the sacraments. This, however, in different ways: for the linking up which is by faith takes place through an act of the soul, while the linking up which is by the sacraments takes place through the use of external things."[1]

It is a favorite idea with Saint Thomas, that faith is truly a contact with Christ, a real, psychological contact with Christ, which, if once established, may lead man into the innermost glories of Christ's life. Without this contact of faith we are dead to Christ, the stream of His life passes us by without entering into us, as a rock in the midst of a river remains unaffected by the turbulent rush of waters. This contact of faith makes man susceptible to the influences of Christ; under normal conditions it will develop into the broader contacts of hope and charity; but it is the first grafting of man on Christ which underlies all other fruitfulness. Till faith be established the great redemption has not become our redemption; the riches of Christ are not ours in any true sense; we are members of the human race, but we are not members of Christ.

It does not belong to my subject to enter into a discussion as to the reasons why one man has faith while another is without faith; nor do I propose to lay down what is that minimum of faith which is indispensable in order to establish true contact between the soul and Christ. It is sufficient for our purpose to know that a man who has faith has laid his hand on the salvation of Christ. It is the most universal way of coming into touch with the redemption of the Cross; it is a way of approach which is always open, in the past, in the present, in the future. Mary, the Mother of God, through her faith, entered into Christ's passion in the very moment of time when it took place; Adam, in his very fall, plunged into it headlong; and it will be present to the last human generation through that wonderful act of the soul of which Saint Thomas speaks in the above text. Whether we say that Christ will suffer—*passurus est*—or whether we say that Christ has suffered—*passus est*—is quite immaterial to the immediateness of contact by faith. "As the ancient Fathers were saved through faith in the Christ to come, so are we saved through faith in the Christ who has already been born and has suffered."[2]

I feel that we are less habituated in our times to think of faith as a kind of psychic link between the soul and Christ; yet such is the traditional concept of that wonderful gift. Anyone who has faith is in the supernatural state, and therefore is directly in touch with Christ's life, even though he be actually in a state of mortal sin.

The Council of Trent has taken great trouble to make clear this point of Catholic moral theology. A man ceases to be Christ's solely through the sin of infidelity; he does not cease to be Christ's through any other sin, however heinous. As long as his faith is a true faith he remains a member of Christ's mystical Body, though there be grievous sores of mortal sin upon his soul. Through that faith, which nothing can kill except the sin of formal infidelity, he keeps so near to the mystery of Christ's death on the Cross that his recovery from the wounds of sin, however grievous, is a normal process of supernatural life, not strictly miraculous. It is true that the faith of the believing Christian in the state of mortal sin is a *fides informis*, a faith devoid of the higher vitalities of charity, yet it is a real faith. Unless we grasp that function of faith as the psychic link between Christ and the soul Catholicism becomes unintelligible. The Church would become, as it did in Lutheran theology, an adventitious association of the elect. But the Church is constituted primarily through faith, and her powers are meant for those who possess that supernatural responsiveness of soul. If we really believe that the Church possesses enough power to wipe away sin, we assume, as well, that sin is compatible with membership in Christ's mystical Body.

Incorporation into Christ, according to Saint Thomas, has a threefold degree; the first is through faith, the second is through the charity of this life, the third is through the possession of heaven.[3] It is true that the whole tendency of faith is towards charity, that ultimately faith without charity cannot save us; nonetheless, charity cannot exist in man without faith, while there may be true faith in man without actual charity.

All this goes to demonstrate that there is in faith an instrumental power, enabling man to open the door that leads to perfect union with Christ. We cannot speak of such instrumental power in charity, for charity is not a means towards the possession of God; it is, on the contrary, actual possession of God. Saint Thomas calls faith an indispensable endowment of the soul, because it is the beginning or principle of spiritual life.[4]

This peculiar position of faith in the spiritual order as a kind of tool of supreme excellence will be seen in a clearer light when we come to ask ourselves the question whether there be another kind of means for man to get at Christ's redemptive life. Once more let it be emphasized that through the possession of charity we do not only contact Christ, we are actually *in* Christ. Charity is not an instrument, while faith has primarily an instrumental role. Now the sacraments are truly such another set of means for the attainment of that final object, to be united with Christ in charity. The sacraments complete and render more efficacious that instrumentality of faith just spoken of: they do not supersede the instrumentality of faith, but they make it more real, if possible, and certainly more infallible in its effect. The relative position of faith and the sacraments in bringing about man's justification through charity is an interesting theological question of which we shall have more to say by-and-by. The sacraments are essentially sacraments of the faith, *sacramenta fidei*, as Saint Thomas invariably calls them; both faith and sacraments have that power of divine instrumentality which open to man the treasure-house of Christ's redemption.

I cannot end this chapter without quoting from Saint Thomas a beautiful passage in which he describes God's action, which he calls grace, keeping faith alive in the soul, even of the sinner:

> Grace produces faith not only when faith begins to exist in the soul for the first time, but also while it habitually abides in the soul.... God brings about the justification of man in the same way as the sun produces light in the air. Grace, therefore, when it strikes with its rays the one who is already a believer is not less efficacious than when it comes for the first time to the unbeliever, because in both it is its proper effect to produce faith: in one case strengthening it and giving it increase, in the other case creating it as an entirely new thing.[5]

The sun of divine grace once above the horizon sends forth its rays of faith into the minds of men, and nothing can resist their light except blind obstinacy and infidelity.

2

Sacraments

There is an excellent definition of the
nature of the sacraments in Article Four of the Sixty-First
Question of the Third Part of the *Summa Theologica*: "Sacraments are certain signs protesting that faith through which man
is justified."[6] Such a definition makes the transition from the role
of faith to the role of the sacraments a very natural and easy
one. The power of the sacraments could never be dissociated
from the power of faith; the two supernatural agencies move
forward hand in hand. A sacrament is always an external sign
witnessing to that more recondite quality of the soul, the faith
that justifies man by bringing him into contact with Christ.

Two very important questions arise here: First, why should
there be this external protestation of the faith? Second, to what
extent shall we give to those signs a literal efficacy of signification? In the answer to the second question there lies all the
difference between Catholicism and Protestantism; in fact, it
may even be said, between Judaism and Christianity. In its
many aspects this will be the main object of our study; but for
the moment let us dwell on the first point, the radical oneness
of the Catholic theory concerning the means of justification.

Faith and sacraments are indissolubly united; though faith

may be called the older and more universal factor. The sacramental system is grafted on faith; it is essentially the executive of our faith; it is, shall we say, the reward of faith. Because of her faith the Church is granted those further powers of reaching Christ which make Christ not only the object of devout contemplation, but of physical possession; the sacramental reality is granted to those who have faith; such is the burden of Christ's teaching in the sixth chapter of Saint John's Gospel. He who does the work of God by believing in Him whom the Father has sent is the one to whom Christ will give His Flesh to eat and His Blood to drink. We may apply here that important principle of spiritual growth which Christ enunciates more than once: "To every one that hath shall be given, and he shall abound, but from him that hath not, that also which he seemeth to have shall be taken away."[7]

Because of her generous faith the Church is given the abundant riches of the sacraments. What might appear at first sight to be the exception to the rule—that faith and the sacraments are indissolubly united—is only a more profound application of it; I refer to the practice of infant Baptism. Saint Thomas, following Saint Augustine, relies on the faith of the Church herself in order to keep intact the essential union of faith and the sacrament of faith. "In the Church of the Saviour the little ones believe through others, as through others they contract those sins which are washed out in Baptism"; these are the words of the earlier Father which the medieval Doctor expands into the following theological explanation: "The faith of one, nay of the whole Church, is of profit to the little one through the operation of the Holy Spirit, who makes the Church into one, and makes the one share the goods of the other."[8] There could hardly be a more unfair accusation brought against the Catholic Church than to say that by her uncompromising insistence on the sacramental life she diminishes the power of faith.

It is really the Puritan, rather than the Protestant in general, who is the enemy of the sacramental system taken in the wider aspect of that Thomistic definition with which we opened this chapter. For the Puritan, faith is not in need of any help or any adjuncts. Yet the reasons given by Catholic theologians for the presence in the Christian dispensation of these external signs of internal faith are chiefly psychological; man's nature being what it is, sacraments are indispensable to a full life of faith.

Saint Thomas gives a threefold reason for the institution of the sacraments;[9] but this threefold reason is really one—man's psychology. However, the three factors are firstly, the condition of man's nature, being a composite of spirit and sense; secondly, man's estate, which is slavedom to material things and only to be remedied by the spiritual power inside the material thing; thirdly, man's activities, so prone to go astray in external interests, finding in the sacraments a true bodily exercise which works out for salvation. Nothing would be easier than to develop this subject with all the fascinating means that psychological studies put at our disposal. The sacramental life of the Church is based on a perfect understanding of man's needs. Sacraments are through their very nature an extension of the Incarnation, a continuation of that mystery expressed in the words: "And the Word was made flesh and dwelt among us." Is not the Son of God made Man, the Sacrament *par excellence*, the *magnum sacramentum*, the invisible made visible? "And evidently great is the mystery of godliness, which was manifested in the flesh, was justified in the spirit, appeared unto angels, hath been preached unto the Gentiles, is believed in the world, is taken up in glory."[10]

To say that a Sacrament is a protestation of the faith which is in us, is not a complete definition of the Christian sacrament; though it may be considered as adequate enough for a sacrament in its widest meaning. Even Saint Thomas never hesitates to give to some of the major rites of the Old Law the name of sacrament; always making it quite clear, however, that the power of those ancient observances never went beyond signifying the patriarchal faith, while the Christian sacrament has a much higher degree of signification, one indeed that has effectiveness associated with it. It would be quite mistaken, and very ungenerous, not to grant to the ancient rites instituted by God sacramental dignity of at least an inferior degree; they all were external signs of the faith in the coming redemption. They were tremendous helps to that faith, although in themselves they were not direct causes of grace.

Saint Thomas divides the life of mankind into four seasons—the state of innocence before the fall, the state of sin before Christ, the state of sin after Christ, and the state of bliss in heaven. No sacraments are necessary in the first and in the last state; sacraments are necessary to man in the two middle states. But it is in the "state of sin after Christ" that sacraments reach their perfection; the seven sacraments of the Christian dispensation are sacraments in the highest sense, because, besides signifying the grace which is the inheritance of faith, they also contain that grace and cause it.[11]

An objector may find fault with the arrangement that God has given to man different sacraments before Christ and different sacraments after Christ. Does this not argue mutability in the divine will? The answer of Saint Thomas is a perfect synthesis of that broader view of the sacramental system which makes it as old as the world:

> To the third objection let us reply that the father of the family
> is not said to be of changeable disposition because he gives
> different orders to his household according to the variety of

seasons, and does not command the same work to be done in summer and in winter; so likewise there is not mutability in God's ways because He institutes one set of sacraments after the coming of Christ and another in the time of the Old Law; for these latter were apt prefigurements of grace, while the former are manifest grace already present amongst us.[12]

3

The Power of
Sacramental Signification

It is the very essence of a sacrament to be a sign; it is its proper definition. "We now speak specifically of sacraments insofar as they imply the relationship of a sign."[13] Let us never deprive a sacrament, even the most excellent, of this constitutional property of signification. The orthodox realist in sacramental theology boldly proclaims his faith, I do not say in the symbolical nature of the sacrament, but in the demonstrative nature of the sacrament as a sign, or, if we like the word better, in its representative nature as a sign. As we shall see by-and-by, this power of signification inside the one and the same sacrament is not simple but complex, for the sacramental element performs its function in various ways, as well as signifying various realities; yet it has a certain definiteness, a clearly outlined circle of signification, which has been traced by the hand of God. It is the divine institution which is directly responsible for the choice of those signs which, in the words of Saint Thomas, are given us "for a more explicit signification of Christ's grace, through which the human race is sanctified."[14] The angelic Doctor adds, with that true liberality of mind so characteristically his own, that this clear circumscribing of the sacramental signs does not in any way narrow the road of salvation, because the material things which are indispensable for the sacraments are commonly to be had, or may be procured with very little trouble.[15]

Sacraments, then, are truly signs from heaven. In no other sphere of human transactions does the external sign become such an efficient messenger of the internal reality. There is in Article Three of the same Question a passage of Saint Thomas which may be called truly classical as stating the power of signification proper to the sacraments; its importance justifies me in giving the Latin first, in spite of its length, to be followed by a translation:

Respondeo dicendum, quod, sicut dictum est, sacramentum proprie dicitur quod ordinatur ad significandam nostram sanctificationem, in qua *tria* possunt considerari: videlicet ipsa *causa* sanctificationis nostrae, quae est passio Christi; et *forma* nostrae sanctificationis, quae consistit in gratia et virtutibus; et ultimus *finis* sanctificationis nostrae, qui est vita aeterna. Et haec omnia per sacramenta significantur. Unde sacramentum est et signum rememorativum ejus quod praecessit, scilicet passionis Christi, et demonstrativum ejus quod in nobis efficitur per Christi passionem, scilicet gratiae, et prognosticum, idest praenuntiativum futurae gloriae.

My answer is, that, as has been already said, the sacrament, properly so-called, is a thing ordained to signify our sanctification; in which *three* phases may be taken into consideration, namely: the cause of our sanctification, which is the passion of Christ; the *essence* of our sanctification, which consists in grace and virtue; and then the ultimate *goal* of our sanctification, which is eternal life. Now all these are signified by the sacraments. Therefore a sacrament is a commemorative sign of what has gone before, in this case the passion of Christ, a demonstrative sign of what is being effected in us through the passion of Christ, that is grace, and a prognostic sign, foretelling our future glory.[16]

Every sacrament, then, has something to declare: it recalls the past, it is the voice of the present, it reveals the future. If the sacrament did not fulfill its function of sign proclaiming something which is not seen, it would not be a sacrament at all. It can embrace heaven and earth, time and eternity, because it is a sign; were it only a grace it would be no more than the gift of the present hour; but being a sign the whole history of the spiritual world is reflected in it: "For as often as you shall eat this bread and drink the chalice, you shall show the death of the Lord, until He come."[17] What Saint Paul says of the Eucharist about its showing forth a past event is true in other ways of every other sacrament. The passage we have transcribed from Saint Thomas refers to every one of the seven sacraments.

In order to elucidate this all-important role of signification in the sacraments we may make a comparison with the non-sacramental means of grace. If my heart be touched by God's grace, such a divine action, excellent and wonderful though it be, is not a sign of anything else; it is essentially a spiritual fact of the present moment, and ends, as it were, in itself. It has no relationship of signification to anything else, whether past, present or future. Such is not the case with the sacraments; through them it becomes possible to focus the distant past and future in the actual present; through them historic events of centuries ago are renewed, and we anticipate the future in a very real way. All this is possible only in virtue of the sacramental sign, which not only records the distant event, but, somewhat like the modern film, projects it upon the screen of the present.

O sacred Banquet, wherein Christ is received, the memory of His passion is recalled, the soul is filled with grace, and there is given to us a pledge of future glory.[18]

This antiphon from the Office of Corpus Christi, when compared with the above text from the *Summa*, at once betrays its Thomistic origin. But although the Eucharist performs that function of transcendent representation in the spiritual order in a more excellent degree, all the other sacraments do the same in their several ways. All the sacraments enable us to step out of the present.

Much confusion of thought in the doctrine of the sacraments in general, and of the Eucharist in particular, would be spared us if we never let go of that elemental definition of the sacrament, that it is a sign. Whatever reality there is in a sacrament is deeply modified by this role of signification. Baptism, for instance, is not just any kind of cleansing of the soul; its cleansing power is in the burial and resurrection of Christ which is signified in the sacramental rite.

Know you not that all we who are baptized in Christ Jesus are baptized in His death? For we are buried together with Him by baptism into death: that, as Christ is risen from the dead by the glory of the Father, so we also may walk in newness of life. For if we have been planted together in the likeness of His death, we shall be also in the likeness of His resurrection.[19]

In this text of Saint Paul the elements of past, present and future in our baptismal conformation with Christ are strikingly verified.

The current definition of a sacrament as an external sign of internal grace would certainly be too narrow for Saint Thomas, if by "internal grace" we meant nothing but the actual transformation of the soul. This is, in fact, only one of the things signified. But if by "internal grace" we also mean the cause of grace—Christ's passion, and the goal of grace—eternal life, then the definition is adequate. But to limit the sacramental power of signification to the present moment, to the transformation of soul which takes place when the sacrament is received, would be an unwarranted minimizing of the sacramental doctrine, and would leave much of our scriptural language unintelligible. How, for instance, could the Eucharist be a memorial of Christ if it were only a supernatural feeding of the soul? When Our Lord said: "Do this for a commemoration of Me,"[20] He gave the Eucharist an historic import which is not to be found in the spiritual raising up of the individual soul alone. A commemoration is essentially a sign, a monument, something related to a definite person or event of the past.

Saint Thomas lays it down as an axiom that a sacrament is always an object of the senses.[21] A merely spiritual thing, an act of our intellect or will, could never fulfill that role of signification which is so essential to the sacrament.[22] The sign, on the contrary, is an external manifestation of the process of thought and volition: Saint Thomas quotes from Saint Augustine a very succinct definition: "A sign is that which, besides the impression it makes on the senses, puts one in mind of something else."

When I see the baptismal water poured on the head of the catechumen, and when I hear the words of the priest who does the christening, if I am a man of faith, my mind, roused by these external rites and signs, travels a long way. I go back to the Jordan, where Christ is being baptized; I go back to Calvary, where blood and water issue from the side of Christ; my mind leaps forward to that people who stand before the Throne of God in white robes which have been washed in the Blood of the Lamb; and, more audacious still, my mind gazes right into the innermost soul of the catechumen and distinguishes that soul from all non-baptized souls, through that spiritual seal which makes it a member of Christ. The sacramental sign is pregnant with all that spiritual vision of my faith. In the order of signs, of course, we include words as well as things; both are, in fact, objects of our senses, and the words are generally necessary to make more precise the signification of the thing. "A repetition of words, when words are added to the visible things in sacraments, is not superfluous, because one receives determination through the other."[23]

In a text already quoted Saint Thomas makes a clear-cut distinction between the two roads which lie before us, and which lead directly to the passion of Christ: the act of the soul, and the use of external things.[24] The former is faith, the latter is the sacrament. Let us give this distinction its full value. The external things are as solid a road to Christ as the act of the soul. The sacramental signs, which are the external things alluded to by the Angelic Doctor, have become, in God's Providence, a distinct supernatural world, as real as the supernatural world of graces given to the souls of men. At the same time, those sacred signs differ radically from the acts of man's soul performed under the inspiration of the Holy Spirit. They are visible, palpable realities, not breathings of the Spirit in the hearts of men. They are not mere aids to man's memory; they are not just opportune reminders of the invisible. "If anyone says that sacraments have been instituted solely for the purpose of fostering faith, let him be anathema."[25] External things have been taken hold of by God as directly as men's souls. Like this visible planet of ours, the supernatural world of salvation is divided into land and water. The graces of the Holy Spirit are the water; the external things, the sacraments, are the land.

4

The Perfection of
Sacramental Signification

It would argue feeble loyalty to Catholic truth if the Protestant abuse of the notion of sacramental signification were to upset the Catholic theologian, and make him too timid to proclaim the marvels of those divine signs. We Catholics, more than anyone else, believe that sacraments are signs, commemorations, monuments of the past. If we neglected this aspect, while trying to save the notion of sacrament, we should be destroying its very nature and making it a thing entirely of the spirit. This would be to go out into the night of Protestantism through another door.

The sacraments are signs of God's action; they are perfect signs because they contain and they bring about the very thing they signify.

> The sacraments of the New Law are at the same time causes and signs; and on this account it is commonly said that they bring about what they signify. From this it also appears that they are sacraments in the most perfect sense of the word, because they are related to something sacred, not only under the aspect of sign, but also under the aspect of cause.[26]

In this they differ profoundly from the sacraments of the Old Law. "The sacraments of the Old Law had no power in themselves by which they might have brought about the bestowal of justifying grace, but they only signified that faith through which men were justified."[27] "But our Sacraments not only contain grace, they cause it."[28] These terse phrases of Saint Thomas express the essence of Catholic doctrine.

The wonderful signs we call sacraments are not only powerful in reminding us of the things of God, they have power to make them live again. They are instruments of the almighty power of God; they are tools in the hands of Christ, "who worketh until now." This is the profound Thomistic concept of the sacraments, that they are the *instrumenta Dei* for bringing about supernatural effects, so that they may be truly called containers of grace.

For Saint Thomas this idea of divine instrumentality is the concept that unites the roles of sign and of cause in one. A tool is a cause through its very nature; a tool may be a sign, too, if it is such as to be obviously most fitted for the work it is expected to do. Is not the sword an emblem as well as an instrument of death? The man who approaches me with a naked sword proclaims my fate as well as executes it. "An instrumental cause, if it be manifest, may be said to be the sign of a hidden effect in that it is not only cause, but also in a way effect, inasmuch as it is wielded by the principal agent."[29] The man who handles a naked sword is indeed the principal cause of my fear. I am not afraid of a sword when not held in a man's grip; nor am I afraid of a human hand without that terrible prolongation of steel; but man and sword together are fearsome, both as a cause and sign. The sword is a dread token of that violence which my enemy intends when he bears down upon me.

But let us leave this gruesome example and come to our

own brighter sphere of sacramental symbols. The waters of Baptism, with the words that go with them, proclaim the mystery of purification, of spiritual cleansing. By themselves they would be only a vague sign; but in the last analysis those waters are poured out by the hand of Christ, and those words are spoken by His mouth; they are truly His tools, as Saint Thomas constantly reminds us; by means of them Christ literally cleanses, no longer the body, but the soul. "That He might sanctify it (the Church), cleansing it by the laver of water in the word of life."[30]

Signification and causation of the spiritual thing, of the mystery of faith, are indissolubly united in the Christian sacrament. If the sacrament were only the signification, it would not rise above the ancient rites of the Jewish Law; if, on the other hand, a sacrament were causation only, it would at once lose its historic value, it would no longer be a reviving of the past, it would have nothing to connect it with the great historic event of Christ's death. Is it not the burden of every page of the *Summa* which deals with the sacraments that they are representations of the death of Christ? Whenever the sacramental doctrine is either falsified or deflected from sound tradition the cause has been this, that men, who ought to have known better, in one way or another ceased to visualize the double concept of signification and causation. The two concepts are strictly inseparable in this matter of the sacrament. The sacrament must be cause in such wise as actually to represent the past, the present, and the future; and it must be sign in such wise as actually to effect the thing which it proclaims.

For the sake of giving a clear example I may be allowed to anticipate my main theme. The Eucharist would not be a sacrament if it were not causative, a bringing about again of the mystery of the death of Christ; nor would it be a sacrament if that mystery of the death of Christ thus brought about in the Eucharist were not done under signs and symbols.

Let us make an extremely bold hypothesis, to elucidate this point. If the priest at the altar brought down Christ from heaven in His natural state as a full-grown man, this would not be a sacrament at all, for the event would lack the very essence of the sacrament, representative signification. We can never insist enough on this aspect of sacramental theology: before all things and above all things we are dealing with signs and symbols, not with things in their own proper nature, *in propria specie*. The Eucharist, being the most perfect sacrament, is more thoroughly representative than any other. At no time in the eucharistic mystery do we deal with Christ in His natural condition, *in propria specie*. It might almost be said that if at any moment in the sacramental process, Christ in His natural condition were to step in, the sacrament would at once be made meaningless. He must be there *in specie aliena*—in a condition different from His natural one—in order to safeguard the character of the sacrament as a sign.

At the same time these signs and symbols, which are the constitutional elements of the sacramental world, are most powerful instruments in the hand of God. They are His tools; they are like the metal disc of a seal in His hand, which, under the pressure of His omnipotence, makes the mystery of faith appear in relief, were it even the Body and Blood of Christ.

If we were met by Christ in Person in our churches, such gracious encounters would have nothing in common with what is called the sacramental Presence. His Presence in the sacrament must be truly such that at no time could it be seen otherwise than by the eye of faith. One is justified in saying that it is the very condition of the sacramental Presence to transcend all vision and all experience even of the highest order, because there is really no kind of perceptive power in man, or even in angel, capable of reacting to that state of being which is proper to the sacrament.

Saint Thomas has thought it worth his while to devote an Article to this very subject: "Whether the Body of Christ as It is in this sacrament can be seen by any eye, at least one glorified?" "The Body of Christ," he answers,

> according to the mode of being which It has in this sacrament, cannot be detected, either by the senses or by imagination, but only through the intellect, which is called the spiritual eye. It is, however, detected by various intellects in various degrees. As the mode of being according to which Christ is in this sacrament is entirely supernatural, Christ is visible to the supernatural intellect only, I mean, the divine intellect; and, as a consequence, to the beatified intellect, either of angel or man, which in a participated brightness of the divine intellect sees the supernatural things in the vision of the divine essence; but as for the intellect of man here on earth, it cannot perceive [the sacramental Presence of Christ] otherwise than by faith, as is the case with all other supernatural things; nor is the angelic intellect capable of seeing it, left to its merely natural resources.[31]

5

Sacramental Thought

The sacramental world is a new world created by God, entirely different from the world of nature and even from the world of spirits. It would be poor theology to say that in the sacraments we have here on earth modes of spiritual realities which resemble the ways of the angels. We have nothing of the kind. Were we to speak with the tongues of angels it would not help us in the least to express the sacramental realities. Sacraments are a unique creation with entirely new laws. They belong to "the mystery which has been hidden from eternity in God who created all things: that the manifold wisdom of God may be made known to the principalities and powers in heavenly places through the church."[32] The creative power of symbols, the productive efficacy of signs, the incredible potentialities of simple things in the hand of God to produce spiritual realities, nay even to reproduce them in their historic setting: all this belongs to the sacramental world and makes it profoundly unlike anything else in heaven or on the earth.

It would be a great disparagement of the sacraments to look upon them as mere veils of more substantial spiritual realities. They are not veiling anything; they are complete realities in themselves, existing in their own right. They are not *infima et infirma elementa*, weak and mean shadows of things; they are the virtue of God and the power of God.

> Our bodily eye is prevented from seeing the Body of Christ through the sacramental species under which it exists, not only as by a covering (as we cannot see what is concealed under a veil), but because the Body of Christ has its relationship to the medium which surrounds this sacrament, not through its proper accidents, but through the sacramental species.[33]

Sacraments have a mode of existence of their own, a psychology of their own, a grace of their own. If they are not beings in the sense in which man is a being or an angel is a being, they are beings nevertheless, resembling God's nature very closely. There is, no doubt, a constant tendency with us to classify the sacraments under the familiar categories of human concepts; but let us remember that sacramental thought is something quite *sui generis*, and the less anthropomorphism, or even the less spiritism, be introduced into it, the better for our theology. Even a master in Israel may well be astonished at the novelty of the life-giving power in the sacrament:

> Jesus answered and said to him: Amen, amen, I say to thee, unless a man be born again, he cannot see the kingdom of God. Nicodemus saith to Him: How can a man be born when he is old? Can he enter a second time into his mother's womb and be born again? Jesus answered: Amen, amen, I say to thee, unless a man be born again of water and the Holy Spirit, he cannot enter into the kingdom of God. That which is born of the flesh is flesh: and that which is born of the Spirit is spirit. Wonder not that I said to thee: You must be born again. The Spirit breatheth where He will and thou hearest His voice: but thou knowest not whence He cometh and whither He goeth. So is everyone that is born of the

Spirit. Nicodemus answered and said to Him: How can these things be done? Jesus answered and said to him: Art thou a master in Israel and knowest not these things?[34]

The sacraments have opened new vistas for human thought, and it is not without spiritual loss that men, no doubt with the best of intentions, speak of them in terms which are applicable only to natural conditions, of man, of angel, even of Christ Himself. To state the Eucharist, for example, in phrases which can only be true of Christ's natural life, is to relinquish a whole new world of divine revelation. Sacraments are not substitutes for anything else, they are their own end and justification. They produce their own grace, and in a way entirely different from all the other modes of participating in the divine life. "The sacrament is achieved," says Saint Thomas, "not through the justice of the man who either gives or receives it, but through the power of God."[35]

Elsewhere he states in terse philosophical language the profound originality of the sacramental concept.

A sacrament of the New Law is an instrumental cause of grace. Therefore grace is in a sacrament of the New Law, not indeed according to a likeness of species, as an effect is in an univocal cause; nor according to any kind of form which is proper, permanent, and proportionate to such an effect, as effects are contained in causes not univocal, as, for instance, things which are generated are in the sun. But grace is contained in the sacrament of the new law according to a certain instrumental power which is transient, and incomplete as a natural being.[36]

To make clear this piece of philosophy, which is truly a golden key to the understanding of the sacramental reality, let us put it more colloquially. Man begets his own offspring in full similarity of nature—that is to say, the child is as truly man as the father. The sun, which is the source of heat and light, is credited by the scholastic thinker with wonderful power of generating life on our planet. The sun is indeed an important contributory cause of the vegetation in our meadows, but it is not their univocal cause, because the big sun does not beget small suns here on earth; it brings out forms of life very different from the constituent elements of the sun. A sacrament is like neither of these; it not only brings about effects which are utterly dissimilar, but it causes without any of that permanent and proportionate vigor which is, for example, in the sun. It has no such permanent and natural fixity of being. If a sacrament were a fixed being in its natural condition, radiating forth grace and life, it would not be a sacrament. With all its realism, a sacrament is a power which is transient, and incomplete as a natural being.[37] I do not apologize to my readers for making this appeal to their highest reasoning powers in order to establish a truth which will be such a gain to them. In sacraments we deal with realities which one might call elusive, in the sense that we can never say of any sacrament that it is either Christ or Holy Spirit or angel or man in their natural, personal mode of existence; though we may say of the sacrament that it can be Christ Himself, if necessary. But then it is not the natural Christ, it is the sacramental Christ; which is a very different proposition.

To sum up: our devotion to the sacraments will be all the sounder and much enlarged if we grasp the fact that the kingdom of God may truly be found in those external and insignificant elements because they are the signs of spiritual things; but signs, as we have so often said, full of divine efficacies: "Things of the senses looked upon in their own nature have nothing to do with the cult of the kingdom of God; but the kingdom of

God is found in them only because they are signs of spiritual things."[38]

May it not be said that the radical difference between Catholicism and Protestantism is in this: that Protestantism is blind to the things of that intermediate world which lies between the creature and the uncreated God; the sacramental world, which is neither nature nor divinity, yet which partakes of both? Protestantism ignores, at least to a very great extent, the fact that there are means of sanctification which are not the personal acts of man, but the sacramental effect.

The sacramental world is truly a mystical world in the best sense of the word: it is reality without fixity of being. Any effort we make in order to cultivate sacramental thought will be rewarded with precious fruits in our spiritual life; it will make us into true mystics. Our dear sacraments are truly a stream of life and light: they are unceasing in their operation; they are more like the great natural powers of radiation discovered by modern science than the inert mass that was once thought to constitute our planet. Saint Thomas's description of the sacrament as a *virtus fluens* (transient power) may remind us of the vision of Ezekiel:

> And as for the likeness of the living creatures: their appearance was like that of burning coals of fire, and like the appearance of lamps. This was the vision running to and fro in the midst of the living creatures, a bright fire and lightning going forth from the fire. And the living creatures ran and returned like flashes of lightning.[39]

The stream of sacramental grace is truly the flow of the Blood of Christ: in one way or another every sacrament is the fire of Christ's love when He was dying on the Cross.

Perhaps the most satisfying line of sacramental thought is to visualize the sacraments as mysterious carriers of all the powers that are in Christ's death. "The power of Christ's passion," says Saint Thomas, "is joined to us (*copulatur nobis*) through faith and through the sacraments, yet in different ways; for the contact (*continuatio*) which is through faith takes place through the act of the soul, but the contact which is through the sacraments takes place through the use of external things."[40]

Let us bear well in mind this wonderful distinction of Saint Thomas. Our personal acts link us up with Christ; in this Catholics and Protestants are agreed. But the use of external things, of the sacramental signs, also links us up with Christ, historically as well as actually. This is as great a phenomenon as the linking up by faith, and in this the Catholic has an enviable certainty of approaching Christ which is denied to the Protestant. This linking up of the sacrament with the real Christ on the Cross is understood by Saint Thomas in a very realistic sense, so much so that according to him the Christian sacrament could not have existed unless Christ Himself had existed in historic time. Faith in Christ could exist before Christ appeared in the reality of the flesh: but the Christian sacrament presupposes the natural and historic presence of Christ on earth. The reason is this, that Christ in His flesh is the effective cause of all the powers that are in the Christian sacrament. Now the effective cause must have a real priority of actual existence: "What does not exist in nature does not put in motion according to the use of external things."[41] A mental act, like that of faith, may precede the event; but signs which are full of actual efficacy receive their power from the historic event or person, and therefore imply the important circumstance that the event has taken place, that the person has lived and died.

Sacraments are truly an energy that comes from Christ in

person, a radiation from the charity of the Cross, a stream of grace from the pierced side of Christ.

> It is manifest that the sacraments of the Church derive their power specifically from the passion of Christ, whose efficacy is linked to us, as it were, through the receiving of the sacraments. As a sign of this, from the side of Christ hanging on the Cross there flowed water and blood, of which the one belongs to Baptism and the other to the Eucharist, which are the two principal sacraments.[42]

6

The Sacramental Role

We are all familiar with the theological adage *Sacramenta sunt propter homines*: Sacraments are for the sake of man. It is a precious maxim which enables us to steer clear of all rigorism in the use of the sacraments; but it must not be thought to express an exclusively utilitarian view of the sacramental system, even within the spiritual order. No supernatural grace could ever be so one-sided. Every grace serves the interests of God as well as the interests of man; it promotes the glory of God as well as the salvation of man. We may accept it as an axiom in the doctrine of grace that man's profit and God's glory are the twofold purpose of one and the same thing, grace. Sacraments would not be the divine things they are if they had not an aspect facing God as well as one turned towards man.

Saint Thomas understood this role well, and he has kept his sacramental doctrine quite free from exclusive spiritual utilitarianism. For him the sacrament is divine cult quite as much as human purification. Let us quote his words:

> The sacramental grace seems to be ordained chiefly for two ends: to remove those defects consequent upon past sins, insofar as they are transitory in act, though they endure in

guilt; and further, to render the soul perfect in those things which belong to the worship of God, according to the Christian religion.[43]

He then goes on to explain that Christ on the Cross destroyed all sin; but that it was also on the Cross that He instituted the rite of the Christian religion, offering Himself as an oblation and victim to God.[44] Sacraments consequently represent the Cross in the double aspect of atonement for sin and worship of God.

It will readily be seen that the introduction of the element of cult into the sacramental system, as its second and nobler half, profoundly modifies sacramental thought. The sacrament, while remaining such, may be worship as much as sanctification; in fact, it is more truly a sacrament through the worship of God than through the sanctification of man. If we go back to the fundamental concept of the sacrament, that it is a representation of Christ's passion, the element of cult is seen to belong to it intrinsically, as it belonged intrinsically to Christ's death on the Cross, which before all things and above all things was a sacrifice to God.

It would be easy to point out this aspect of cult in every one of the sacraments, even were we to leave aside for the moment the Eucharist. Some sacraments emphasize their role of cult more explicitly than others. Saint Thomas thinks that those which imprint a character on the human soul have the element of worship more prominently, always excepting the Eucharist. "In a special way the sacraments which imprint a character on the soul bestow on man a certain consecration, thus deputing him for divine worship; just as inanimate things are said to be consecrated, insofar as they are set aside for divine worship."[45] In an earlier Article of the same Question the Doctor had written succinctly: "Those who are delegated for the Christian cult, whose author is Christ, receive a character, by which they are made conformable to Christ."[46]

The Thomistic view of the sacrament then is clear; it indissolubly unites cult and sanctification; it prepares us for the idea of the Christian sacrifice, which is highest worship, being found in a sacrament; as sacraments are cult, not by a kind of after-thought, but through their first and most conspicuous element. Anyone can easily see what a wide deflection from the sacramental concept it would be if at any time we turned entirely to the left, so to speak, to the element of sanctification, forgetting all about the element of worship. Let us cling to the old maxim *Sacramenta propter homines*, provided we realize that nothing is so useful to man as to adore God. If we let man have the sacraments plentifully, without any stint, it is in order to enable him, before all things and above all things, to perform the rites of the Christian religion. We must ever remember that the sacrament is a *res sacra*—a sacred thing—given to man so as to enable him to approach God. It is the cup of sacrificial blood which man holds in his hand so that he may have the right of entering into the Holy of Holies. In the sacramental system man is active, not only passive; in it he gives back to God God's own gifts.

I do not speak here of those acts that may be necessary on the part of man to make him a fit recipient of the sacrament: such are more truly called dispositions or predispositions. I am now alluding to the real sacramental activity of which Saint Thomas speaks so much.

A sacrament may belong to the divine cult in three ways; first, by way of the thing done, second, by way of the agent, third, by way of the recipient. By way of the action itself, the Eucharist belongs to the divine cult because in that sacrament divine worship is found in a supreme manner, as it is the sacrifice of the Church.... As for agents in the sacraments, we have the sacrament of Order, because through this sacrament men are delegated to confer the sacrament on others. Pertaining to recipients, however, we have the sacrament of Baptism, because through this is conferred on man power of receiving the other sacraments of the Church, whence it is called the door of the sacraments. To this latter class also belongs the sacrament of Confirmation.[47]

In all this we clearly perceive the trend of Saint Thomas's theology. Sacraments are activities, even on the part of man, because they are either the divine cult itself, or man's sanctification for the divine cult. It would certainly be an impoverishment of the sacramental system if in it man were merely passive, were nothing but a recipient; the sacraments would lack the fire of life, the exhilaration of generous action.

Before entering into the heart of our subject we ought to examine the special function of sacramental grace in the growth of human sanctity. "The sacramental grace," says Saint Thomas, "adds to grace commonly so called, over and above the virtues and gifts, a certain divine help which enables man to reach the end of the sacraments."[48] Saint Thomas makes the sacramental grace a kind of species under the larger genus of grace.[49] Let us keep in mind this individual character of each sacrament. There is no overlapping in their activities; there is no confusion in their respective roles; they are not interchangeable in their purpose; they are as completely different in their spiritual results as they are different in their external symbols. The water of Baptism, the bread and wine of the Eucharist, and the chrism of Confirmation are very different elements indeed; but they do not differ from each other more than the internal effects of their respective sacramental powers.

The sacramental graces are specially characterized by their

intimate connection with Christ's passion and death. They are not just any grace, but grace as flowing from the pierced side of Christ. "Why is it," asks Saint Thomas, "that Baptism washes away, even in the old sinner who approaches it, every stain of sin and all the guilt of sin besides?" "The suffering of the passion of Christ is communicated to the one who is baptized, inasmuch as he becomes a member of Christ, as if he himself had borne that pain, and therefore all his sins are remitted through the pain of Christ's passion."[50]

In the body of the same Article he had stated this truth, even more tersely:

> In Baptism man is incorporated into the passion and death of Christ, according to Romans 6:8: *If we be dead with Christ, we believe that we shall live also with Christ.* It is clear, then, that to everyone who is baptized the passion of Christ is communicated as a healing power, as if he himself had suffered and died.

Could the sacramental grace be summed up more gloriously? The privilege of the baptized is "as if he himself had suffered and died"![51]

7

The Sacramental Setting of the Eucharist

We need not regret having spent so much time trying to master the salient points of the Church's sacramental doctrine. Nothing could be more futile than an attempt to understand the Christian Eucharist without this previous education in the broader concepts of sacramental theology. The Eucharist is a sacrament; it is nothing but a sacrament; and it is set like a jewel in the very midst of the marvelous sacramental system. *Tantum ergo sacramentum veneremur cernui* (Down in adoration falling, Lo! the sacred Host we hail) is the most popular, as well as the most technically exact, expression of Catholic admiration for the great gift of the Eucharist; humbly and gratefully we prostrate ourselves before the Holy Sacrament on our altars.

It is certainly the great merit of Saint Thomas that he has found it possible to give an absolutely complete exposition of the Eucharist without ever departing from these fundamental sacramental concepts. He lays the foundations of sacramental theology in general so broadly that at no time is he compelled to buttress the glories of any of the seven sacraments with outside considerations, speculations or theories. High as the sacrament may rise, it is built up from the common sacramental foundation.

The Blessed Eucharist reaches the very Throne of God; it is more than the food of the soul giving immortality, it is the Blood of the New Covenant, it is the sacrifice of the Lamb unspotted. But all these splendors, unexpected as they may seem, do not take Saint Thomas by surprise; they belong to the sacrament; they can be stated in sacramental terms, and the Eucharist in its double aspect of cult and food, of sacrifice and communion, does not in that respect differ from the other six sacraments, rather is it the sacrament *par excellence*. It is the first of the sacraments, not because at any point it breaks through the divine circle of sacramental significance, but because from within that great circle it rises to the Throne of God. "The Eucharist is the perfect sacrament of the Lord's passion inasmuch as it contains the very Christ Himself who suffered."[52]

We distinguish in the Eucharist between the sacrifice and the communion; we even speak of the faithful who receive holy communion, as "receiving the sacrament," thus introducing into theological language a workable distinction between the Eucharist as sacrifice and the Eucharist as sacrament. Saint Thomas himself, with all his grasp of the oneness of the Eucharistic sacrament, uses this duality of expression when necessary. I shall have more to say on this presently, but let it be clear at once that this is merely a necessity of language, which has nothing in common with the much more drastic divisions of sacrifice and sacrament which were introduced at a later date.

Indeed it would be truly disastrous if at any time we came to look upon the Eucharist in its sacrificial aspect as something less sacramental or even non-sacramental, reserving the sacramental denomination exclusively for the reception of Christ's

Body and Blood. This would at once remove the Eucharistic sacrifice from the sacramental system of the Church, though it would leave it as something for which there are no provisions in our general theology. It would set it apart as something unique, with no universal idea to explain it or hold it within the general scheme of sanctification. Saint Thomas would have been the very last man to make such a blunder; for him, and in fact for the whole age in which he lived and taught, the Eucharistic sacrifice is an essentially sacramental thing; the Eucharist is a sacrament at its best because it is a ritual offering to God in the New Covenant. At no time did Saint Thomas in his explanation of the Christian sacrifice go outside his general theory of the sacraments. In order to explain sacrifice he never borrows considerations from other parts of theology; the sacramental principle provides him with a key to the mystery of the Mass.

We may make this more clear by comparing the method of Saint Thomas with that of some later theologians. Holding by faith the fact that at Mass the Son of God is offered up under the appearance of bread and wine, these have asked themselves the question: how is Christ in a state of victim on the altar? They have propounded various theories in order to explain this state of immolation; they have suggested, for instance, that Christ's mode of existing under the Eucharistic species represents a sort of abasement or humiliation compared with His natural state of glory.

I do not pretend to criticize such views; I do not deny that the state of abasement may be a state of sacrifice; all that I intend to make clear now is this, that such an explanation of the Eucharistic sacrifice comes not from the center of the sacramental doctrine, but has been brought in from quite another realm of Christian thought; it has been borrowed from the sphere of ethics. Humiliation and exaltation are not sacramental ideas, they are ethical notions. The sacrament is a representation of an historic fact, not an ethical deed which has new meritoriousness. But Saint Thomas never left the straight road of sacramental thought in all his loving considerations of the Eucharistic mystery. This is particularly evident when he considers the Eucharist exclusively from the angle of the ritual sacrifice. Having once grasped the profound fact that the Eucharist is a true sacrament, he never lets go of that idea, and he succeeds in giving us a theology of the Eucharist which is a masterpiece of harmonious thought; he places the sacrament of the altar in the center of the whole sacramental system, and he makes all the other sacraments converge towards it.

We are well aware of the disruption of this harmony at the Reformation, when Protestants denied the sacrificial character of the Eucharist, making the sacrament the merely passive reception of the Body and Blood of Christ. I speak now of Protestantism in its early and less antagonistic period of thought, when it still held the Real Presence. It then became necessary in practice for the Catholic theologians to distinguish in the Eucharist itself between the sacrament and the sacrifice, reserving the term "sacrament" almost exclusively for the receiving of Holy Communion; but this is merely a tactical move which need not mislead us Catholics. The term "sacrament" in fact covers the whole Eucharist as with a golden baldachino of glory; the sacrifice of the Church, Mass, is truly the sacrament at its best and fullest; and the sacrifice of Mass, if it has any human explanation, must be explained in sacramental concepts. Now this is exactly what Saint Thomas achieved; his was a work of genius whose importance is not always appreciated by men even of sincere intentions, yet whose effects are great beyond calculation in the past and future history of theology. The Corpus Christi liturgy sings the glory of the divine sacrifice in sacramental terms, and certainly in practice the Church makes use of her divine treasure, the Eucharistic sacrifice, in a sacramental way, which is indeed a very human way, for as with all the other sacraments it is put at men's disposal with lavish abundance.

It is the main purpose of this book to make clear that in dealing with the Eucharist in all its aspects we are dealing with a sacrament. The rules that govern its use, its frequency, shall I say its proprietary rights, are sacramental rules. In the following chapters we shall let Saint Thomas speak for himself; this present chapter is intended to state the points I wish to emphasize. It will be easy for anyone to perceive at a glance that to restrict our explanation of the Eucharistic mystery, and above all of the Eucharistic sacrifice, to sacramental concepts, is in a way a limitation of the scope of imagination, and certainly a check to devotional exaggeration. Yet let us be quite sure of one thing, that the Eucharist, with all its magnitude, is a very definite thing, as all sacraments are definite things, at no time rendering superfluous any of the other elements of the Christian dispensation.

Three concepts belonging to the general theory of sacraments in the theology of Saint Thomas, more than any others, have made it possible for him to keep the Eucharist entirely within the sacramental circle. (Here I am repeating what we have already said in a previous chapter.) The first, so prolific in its consequences, is the representative signification in every sacrament of a past, a present, and a future; the past being the death of Christ on the cross, the present being the very thing which the external symbol signifies, the future being the union with Christ in glory. The second concept, belonging to the sacraments in general, and as fertile, is this: that the sacrament is not only man's healing but also God's glorification, i.e., the divine cult. It will be readily perceived that the Eucharistic sacrifice which is radically a representative sacrifice of a past immolation, and which is essentially a supreme act of worship, moves easily within such broad views concerning sacraments in general. The third idea, so dear to Saint Thomas, that the sacrament actually contains what it signifies; that it is not merely an external symbol, but a true carrier of spiritual realities. This notion of containing, to which the Doctor clings with such tenacity in his general theory on the sacraments, makes it possible for him to speak of the immolated Christ as being contained in the sacrament, "The sacrament is called a victim (*hostia*) because it contains Christ Himself, who is the victim of salvation."[53]

Saint Thomas calls the Holy Eucharist *The sacrament* by antonomasia. This, we may explain with the help of the Standard Dictionary, is a figure of speech whereby an epithet stands for a proper name, or one individual for a whole species, as incorporating in itself alone the qualities that are to be found throughout the species. In the Article from which I have just quoted an objection had been put forward that most of the names which traditional usage appropriates to the Eucharist might also be applied to other sacraments, and that, consequently, they are not peculiarly characteristic of the Eucharist. All sacraments of the New Law are a good grace (*bona gratia*), so they might all be called a Eucharist; all sacraments help us on the road of life, so they might all be called a viaticum; all sacraments achieve something sacred, so they might all be called sacrifice; in all the sacraments the faithful come together, so they all might be called communion; why, then, reserve the term of Eucharist, of viaticum, of sacrifice, of communion, to one sacrament alone? To which Saint Thomas replies, that whatever is common to all the other sacraments is predicated of this sacrament antonomastically on account of its excellency.[54]

A more telling way there could not be of stating that the Eucharist in all its aspects must remain within the sacramental circle; but let us hear the main doctrine contained in the body of the Article:

> This sacrament has a threefold signification; one with regard to the past insofar as it is commemorative of the Lord's passion, which was a true sacrifice, and according to this it is called a sacrifice; it has a second signification with regard to the present, namely ecclesiastical unity, into which men are incorporated through the sacrament, and according to that aspect it is called communion.... It has a third signification with regard to the future, inasmuch as the sacrament is a figure of the divine fruition which will take place in heaven, and according to this aspect it is called viaticum, because it gives us here on earth the means of getting there. According to this aspect also it is called Eucharist, which means "good grace," because the grace of God is eternal life.[55]

If this is a broad and comprehensive view of the Eucharist it is not more so than the general view of sacramental grace held by Saint Thomas. The difference is not in breadth, but in height and depth. On account of its excellency things are simply truer in the case of the Eucharist; and if, to use a colloquialism, blood is thicker than water, the Eucharistic reality within the sacramental vessel is more effective because it is Blood, the Blood of God Himself.

8

Sacramental Harmony

What I have to say in this chapter is entirely for Catholics, for those who believe all the Church teaches on the Holy Eucharist and on the sacraments generally. My line of argument is frankly *ad hominem*, an appeal to those very truths which we all hold dear. With most Catholics knowledge and appreciation of the Eucharist is in a way clearer and more pronounced than their knowledge and appreciation of the great sacramental system of the Church considered as a whole. The reason of this preference is obvious. In nothing are we more carefully instructed than in all that belongs to the Eucharist; First Communions are quite a social feature in modern Catholicism. Of course this is all to the good, and it is my purpose now to make use of that charisma of our own days, love of the Eucharist, in order to give the sacramental doctrine of the Church, considered in its more universal aspect, the benefit of that familiar knowledge that goes with devotion.

The Eucharist ought really to illuminate for us all the other sacraments with its own radiance. The Eucharist is the sun in the firmament of sacramental grace. Is there not, however, sometimes a danger on the one hand of giving the Eucharist a position such as would hardly retain it in its sacramental setting, while on the other hand there may be the greater peril of our lowering the status of the other sacraments to conventional forms of lesser spiritual power? Yet the Eucharist ought to safeguard for us all the spiritual glories of the other sacraments, by keeping them within the orbit of the divine Presence; while they in turn, being as truly sacraments, although they do not contain the Body and Blood of Christ, will enable us to see even the Eucharist in its true perspective. We may put it in the following way: One sacrament, while remaining entirely a sacrament, and indeed through the very laws of its sacramentality, and not as an unusual feature or external adjunct, contains the true Body and Blood of Christ; it does this in virtue of its sacramental state, not because it is more than a sacrament.

So we turn to the other sacraments and say: If a sacrament may be the Body and Blood of Christ, can we be surprised at anything that may be claimed for any of the other sacraments? After all, they are sacraments in the truest and most literal sense of the word, theirs is not a diminished form of spiritual power; they are all of them the seven spirits of God, sent out over the whole world. Traditional Catholicism loves to keep the seven together, as one family; and the Council of Trent has given them all letters patent of nobility: "If anyone says ... that any of these seven is not truly and properly a sacrament, let him be anathema."[56]

There is of course among the seven a diversity in that which the Council calls dignity, one sacrament possessing greater nobility in the peerage. "If anyone says ... that in no wise is one sacrament of greater dignity than another, let him be anathema."[57] This supreme sacrament is the Blessed Eucharist. Saint Thomas calls it simply *potissimum inter alia sacramenta*, most powerful of all the sacraments. Yet his way of explaining this supremacy of the Eucharist shows clearly how well he understood the whole sacramental system to be one perfect organism, in which the seven arteries of life work in unison. He sees a threefold reason for the supremacy of the Eucharist. "In it Christ is contained substantially, while in the other sacraments there is a certain instrumental power derived from Christ."[58] Again, all the other sacraments prepare men for the Eucharist, and find in it their consummation. Thirdly—and this is the ritual aspect of the sacraments—Catholic practice makes the other sacraments end in the celebration of the Eucharist.[59]

Without being hypercritical, and without finding fault with the ways in which other men's minds work, may I not venture a mild censure of much that is written with a sincere intention of instructing the people of God? We seem to have isolated the Eucharist, making it stand like a cedar of Lebanon in solitary grandeur on the mountaintop, when, with all its wonderful fruitfulness, it is only one of the trees of the supernatural garden of God. It occupies the center, it is surrounded by the six trees that bear fruit unto eternal life; it is not a solitary growth of disproportionate size. We shall understand the Eucharist better if we know much about the other sacraments; and we shall also be taught by the supreme creation, the Eucharist, how to appreciate the other marvels which are its companions.

Even masters in theology have not always recognized as they ought the true harmony of the sacramental system. They accept everything the Church teaches about the Eucharist, about Transubstantiation, about the power of the priest at the altar; they could not refuse the obedience of faith to such doctrines, which embody the intense objective reality of the sacrament of the altar; but for various reasons, which are not relevant to our subject, such men, when they come to the other sacraments, practically reduce them to infallible signs of grace, underestimating in them those qualities of life and power which they have to grant to the Eucharist. This attitude is extremely illogical. Anyone who believes in the Eucharist, as every Catholic theologian does, grants enough to that external thing in the supernatural sphere—the sign, to make him ready for more. If under the appearance of bread and wine there can be the Body and the Blood of Christ, Saint Thomas, the most honest and logical of all thinkers, will say that under baptismal water there also can be the power of the Holy Spirit, so that baptismal water, or any other sacramental sign, is not only an infallible token of God's activity in the souls of men, it is more. Water, chrism, and words of absolution, all contain a participated power from Christ.

"Is the Eucharist a sacrament?" asks Saint Thomas. "As the power of the Holy Spirit is with regard to the water of Baptism, so the true Body of Christ is with regard to the appearance of bread and wine and therefore the species of bread and wine effect nothing except through the power of Christ's true Body."[60] There is, then, a close relationship between the power of the baptismal water and the power of the sacramental Bread; there is truly no abyss between sacrament and sacrament.

The whole sacramental efficiency in the theology of Saint Thomas receives wonderful unity through the doctrine of supernatural instrumentality. All the sacraments, not excepting the Eucharist, considered at least as communion, are like divine tools in the hands of Christ; with them He profoundly stirs the world of souls, and raises it up to the level of God.

"How is it," asks an objector, "that a sacrament in which Christ is received after all under a strange form, *sub specie aliena*, is still capable of bringing man to the possession of Christ in His proper form, *in specie propria*, in heavenly glory?" Answer: "That Christ should be received under a strange form belongs to the very nature of a sacrament, which acts instrumentally. Now nothing prevents an instrumental cause from producing a more powerful effect."[61]

The Eucharist, though it contain the very Body and Blood of Christ, has still only an instrumental causality with regard to eternal glory; and this is the very definition, according to Saint Thomas, of the whole of sacramental causality: it is instrumental in the hands of God. The sacramental thing, the outward sign, receives from God all the powerful energies and delicate precision that an artist puts into the tool with which he carves a statue. In this Saint Thomas recognizes the superiority of the sacrament of the New Law to the sacrament of the Old Law. For him too, the three sacramental characters, of Baptism, Confirmation, and Holy Order, are spiritual instrumentalities through which God operates inside the sacramental system, making the sacrament produce the sacrament.

The official minister of the sacrament is merely an instrument of God.

> The ministers of the Church do not by their own power cleanse men who come to the sacraments, and they do not give grace to them. But Christ by His own power does this through them, as through certain instruments, and therefore the effect which follows, in those who receive the sacrament, is not in the likeness of the ministers, but a configuration to Christ.[62]

By making sacramental ministry another form of divine instrumentality, Saint Thomas has pulled together the whole sacramental system into an indissoluble organism of divine vitality. He is far indeed from that loosely connected and almost disjointed theology of the sacraments which is not an uncommon phenomenon in our days.

The difference between the Eucharist and the other sacraments is, of course, clear to the mind of Saint Thomas; but again he states it sacramentally, not in phrases borrowed from the natural order of things.

A sacrament is so called because it contains something sacred. Now a thing may be sacred in two ways, either absolutely, or with reference to something else. The difference between the Eucharist and the other sacraments which have a matter known to the senses is this, that the Eucharist contains something sacred absolutely, namely Christ Himself; but the water of Baptism contains something sacred with regard to something else, that is to say, it contains the power of sanctifying; and the same thing may be said of the chrism and of the other sacramental things. Consequently, the sacrament of the Eucharist is fully accomplished (*perficitur*) in the very consecration of the matter, while the other sacraments are fully accomplished in the application of the matter to the man to be sanctified.

From this another difference follows; for in the sacrament of the Eucharist what is the "thing and the sacrament" (*res et sacramentum*) is in the matter itself; while what is the "thing only" (*res tantuni*)—i.e., the grace which is given—is in the one who receives the Eucharist; but in Baptism both are in the recipient, that is to say, character, which is the "thing and the sacrament" and the grace of remission of sins, which is the "thing" only, and the same may be said of the other sacraments.[63]

This passage is of such extreme importance in sacramental matters that every theologian ought to know it by heart. Nothing better has been said in the course of centuries on the unity of the sacramental system, with all its diversity of grades of dignity. The fundamental principle, that the Eucharist is complete, is perfectly accomplished in the consecration of the matter, is the basis of all we have to say on the sacramental aspect of Mass; the Consecration is, of course, the complete Eucharist, because it is the perfect memorial of Christ's passion.

Before ending this chapter I must say a few words on the theological distinction here made use of by Saint Thomas, which runs through his whole sacramental doctrine. The Schoolmen made this threefold division: *sacramentum tantum*, the sacrament only; *sacramentum et res*, the sacrament and the thing; *res tantum*, the thing only.

The first, *sacramentum*, is all that we know as the signification, with its divine power and its commemorative affinities. The "sacrament and the thing" is the spiritual inwardness of the whole sacramental signification and no longer the external symbolism. Thus in Baptism the character which is distinct from all the other spiritual results of Baptism would be called by Saint Thomas *sacramentum et res*, because baptismal character, an entirely spiritual result of the external rite, is still a sacramental thing, since in its turn it is a representation of, and a configuration with, the sacerdotal office of Christ, as will be explained later. "Sacrament and thing" thus holds a very important position in the old theology. It is a blending of the internal spiritual reality, *res*, with signification, *sacramentum*. Quite logically, then, Saint Thomas declares in the above passage that in the Eucharist "sacrament and thing" is in the external matter itself, because truly the "thing," the spiritual reality, the Body and Blood of Christ, under the appearance of bread and wine, is also "sacrament"—that is, representative in a new way of the Christ on the Cross, when Body and Blood were separated. Saint Thomas really admits a double signification in the sacraments—at least, in some of them; first, the external thing signifies; and then the internal, spiritual reality, immediately produced by the sacrament, has, in its turn, the role of representation. The Eucharist excels, because in it *sacramentum et res* is not in the recipient, but in the external signs of bread and wine. Here, again, we have a truly sacramental basis for the sacrificial aspect of the Eucharist. Coming now to the *res*—the "thing"—it would not be an accurate reading of the old masters to say that by it is meant grace in general. What is meant is specific, sacramental grace, such as spiritual regeneration in Baptism or the union of charity in the Eucharist, when the faithful receive It in Holy Communion.

The middle member of the threefold division—*sacramentum et res*—is really the most interesting to the theologian, because it means a transposing of sacramental signification into the first spiritual results of the sacrament. For the Eucharist it means that not only the whole external rite of Mass signifies sacrifice, but the consecrated elements, or rather, the infinitely holy Thing under the elements, also signifies sacrifice, as being the immediate representation of Christ immolated on the Cross.

9

The Sacramental Idiom of Saint Thomas

The present chapter is intended to redeem the promise made in a previous one to let Saint Thomas speak for himself. We said that the great Doctor found it possible to state the whole Eucharistic mystery in sacramental concepts. That he did so we now proceed to show. There is this very evident fact that nowhere has Saint Thomas treated the Sacrifice of the Mass as a separate theological subject; in this he stands in striking contrast to later theologians. The Eucharistic sacrifice is entirely subsumed under the concept of the Eucharistic sacrament—nay, more, the Eucharistic sacrament is said by him to have its main expression and celebration in the consecration; which consecration, again, according to him, is the direct and complete sacramental representation of Christ's passion, and as such, is sacrifice.

It will be a simple task to put before the reader a number of evident texts from the *Summa*. There is, first of all, its author's invariable habit of making the term *sacramentum* the subject of every phrase that has anything to do with the Eucharist. He will say that the sacrament is sacrifice; that the sacrament is celebrated at Mass; that to receive the sacrament in communion is a natural outcome of the sacrament; he will even say that the sacrament is at the same time sacrament and sacrifice (sacrament when it is received, sacrifice when it is offered up), suggesting an apparent tautology, which reminds one of the schoolboy's definition of man, when he said that man consists of man and woman. There is no irreverence intended here; indeed we are dealing with a subject in which difficulties of expression make children of us all. When Saint Thomas says that the sacrament is at the same time sacrament and sacrifice he is far from that modern dichotomy which splits the Eucharist into two separate realities; his distinction implies the containing of two things in one—nay, even the containing of a minor thing in a greater thing; the sacrifice is the greater thing which contains the minor thing, the participation. But of this more presently.

Let us see how the word *sacramentum* is for Saint Thomas the subject for everything that is being predicated of the Eucharist, be it sacrifice or communion. An objector says: "This sacrament of the Eucharist ought not to be of profit to anyone except him who receives it, for it belongs to the same genus as the other sacraments: but the other sacraments are of profit only to the one who receives them; the effect of Baptism, for instance, is confined to the baptized person. Therefore this sacrament, too, ought to be considered as profitable only to the one who receives it." The answer is simple and limpid: "This sacrament has this in addition to the others, that it is a sacrifice, and so there is a difference of condition."[64]

To another objector who finds it difficult to reconcile completeness of the sacrament with the Latin practice of communicating under one kind only, Saint Thomas explains that the perfection of the sacrament is not in the use made of it by the faithful, but in the consecration of the matter; for the representation of Christ's passion is enacted in the very consecration of the sacrament.[65] It is evident that for him the sacrament is essentially in the consecration; which again, as Body and Blood are consecrated separately, is essentially the representation of Christ's passion, and therefore a sacrifice.

There is another very clear identification of sacrament and sacrifice. Mass, for Saint Thomas, is simply the sacrament which is being celebrated:

> In Mass there are two things to be considered, namely the sacrament itself, which is the principal thing, and the prayers which are said at Mass for the living and the dead. From the point of view of sacrament, the Mass of a bad priest is not of less value than the Mass of a good priest, because in both cases the same sacrament is being offered.[66]

To offer up Mass then is simply *conficere sacramentum*, to make the sacrament, in the terse but perfectly exact language of the Catholic theologians of the period.

Nothing would be easier for me than to multiply texts of that kind, gleaned from the pages of the *Summa* of Saint Thomas, where he treats of the sacraments and particularly of the Eucharist. All such texts are for the most part *obiter dicta*, casual remarks which show how firmly the idea was embedded in his mind that the celebration of Mass is a sacramental act, and that, in a cherished phrase of his, the Eucharist is celebrated in the consecration more truly than in the communion: "The sacrament is accomplished (*perficitur*) in the consecration of the matter; the use of the sacrament by the faithful does not of necessity belong to the sacrament, but is something following upon the sacrament."[67]

It may be that today our minds are less habituated to the view that the Eucharistic sacrament is chiefly the offering of the sacrifice of Mass; yet there can be no doubt that such was the attitude of mind in the ages of faith, of which Saint Thomas is the finest representative. The use of the sacrament, Holy Communion, is held by him to be something that follows upon a sacramental act which is already complete in the consecration. "The use of the consecrated matter in the Eucharist belongs to a certain perfection of the sacrament, just as operation is not the first, but the second perfection of a thing."[68] The philosophical principle invoked is very apposite. Operation is said to be the second perfection of a thing; for example, a man is perfect man, in the first instance, from having a human nature; to think and act with that nature is the second perfection; yet man is fully man, even when he does not actually think or work. So the Eucharist is fully sacrament the moment it is consecrated. It fulfills its mission then, because then the sacrament-sacrifice is accomplished.

Another beautiful and terse phrase which I cannot resist quoting in this connection is the following: "The use of the sacrament follows this sacrament."[69] In modern terms we would say communion follows Mass; but who does not see how much more accurate is the phrase of Saint Thomas? The sacrament already exists, has accomplished its great mission, has fulfilled its role, before the faithful approach to receive It. Shall we say that the faithful come in at the end of the sacred drama? The sacrament has been completed, has shed its light heavenwards and earthwards, before the faithful eat It, because the sacrifice has been performed once more. If sacrifice and sacrament were not identical, how could it ever be said that the use of the sacrament comes after the sacrament?

It is true that when Saint Thomas comes to treat of the various effects of the great sacrament, then for the first time he seems to be less precise in his terms. He says: "This sacrament is at the same time sacrifice and sacrament; but it has the nature of sacrifice inasmuch as it is offered up, and it has the nature of a sacrament inasmuch as it is partaken."[70] This useful and facile distinction has often been adopted, and it is made use of with great effect by so orthodox a manual as the *Catechism of the Council of Trent*. But the whole context of the *Summa* forbids our confining the sacramental character of the Eucharist exclusively to the *sumptio*, or partaking of the Eucharist. Saint Thomas does not say the Eucharist is sacrament and sacrifice, but he says "this sacrament is sacrament and sacrifice"; the one and the same sacrament has a twofold function: the more common sacramental function of feeding the soul, in which function it resembles all the other sacraments, and which, therefore, may be called directly sacramental, and the function of sacrifice, which is a property exclusive to the Eucharist, and which it is quite legitimate to distinguish from the ordinary function of spiritual feeding without losing in any way its own innate sacramentality.

Let us conclude this study of the mind of Saint Thomas with a more lengthy passage, which not only perfectly illustrates his Eucharistic idiom, but must stimulate our devotion to the blessed sacrament. In the Sixth Article of the Seventy-Third Question he had set out to show that the Paschal Lamb of the Old Law was the most perfect figure of the Eucharistic sacrament in the New.

> In this sacrament we may consider three things: namely, that which is sacrament only, the bread and wine; that which is the thing and sacrament, the true Body of Christ; and what is the thing only, the effect of this sacrament. Now regarding what is sacrament only the perfect figure of this sacrament was the oblation of Melchizedek, who offered bread and wine. In relation to Christ crucified (*Christum passum*), who is contained in this sacrament, its figures were all the sacrifices

of the Old Testament, especially the sacrifice of expiation, which was the most solemn of all. But with regard to the effect, the principal figure of that was the manna, which *had in itself the savor of all sweetness* (Wisdom 16:20), just as the grace of this sacrament refreshes the soul in so many ways.

The Paschal Lamb, however, prefigures this sacrament in a threefold manner: Firstly, inasmuch as it was eaten with unleavened bread, according to Exodus 12:8, *They shall eat the flesh ... and unleavened bread.* Secondly, it was immolated by the entire multitude of the children of God on the fourteenth day of the month; a figure of the passion of Christ, who on account of His innocence was called the Lamb. But with regard to the effect, as by the blood of the Paschal Lamb the children of Israel were protected by the destroying angel, and delivered from the Egyptian captivity, so the Paschal Lamb is the chief figure of this sacrament, for in all like things it foreshadows it.[71]

Not once in this copious analysis does Saint Thomas hesitate to make the word "sacrament" the subject of which so many varied things are being predicated. We may rest assured that we shall be using good Catholic language in preferring to all other terms that of "sacrament" when we speak of the Blessed Eucharist.

Finally, the prayer of the Church comes naturally to our lips: "O God, who in this wonderful sacrament has bequeathed to us a memory of your Passion, grant us, we beseech Thee, so to venerate the sacred mysteries of your Body and Blood that we will continually experience the fruit of your Redemption in us."[72]

10

The Sacramental View of the Sacrifice of the Mass: Its Negative Aspect

In theological matters the spark that illumines always comes from under the hoof of hard thinking. To conceive the sacrifice of Mass as a sacrament is a simple visualization of a great truth which, if it be once grasped by the mind, even were it after a painful logical process, makes all the difference between reality and fantasy. The great Christian sacrifice is essentially a sacramental mystery; this fact we have established to our satisfaction.

Let us now see how such a conclusion affects the working of our faith. I am not yet giving the explanation of the way in which a sacrament can be a sacrifice; this will be our next task; just now I am interested in the mental attitude of one who knows clearly that the sacrifice of Mass is a sacramental thing. I want to speak of that liberty of mind possessed by the Catholic people, those whom Saint Peter calls "a royal priesthood," in their acceptance of one of the most tremendous mysteries ever revealed to man. In believing the divine sacrifice of the Mass to be a sacrament, they must envisage what takes place on the altar in a way which creates a quite unique mentality. They are asked to distinguish two things; first, that on the altar, at a given moment, there is offered up the perfect sacrifice whose elements are absolutely divine, being, in fact the Body and Blood of Christ. But they are not to give to that sacrifice a meaning which is in any way merely natural, as if it were a sacrifice in the sense in which other sacrifices have been offered here on earth, as if that element of destruction were present which has been the common property of all natural sacrifices.

In other words, the principle that in the Mass our sacrifice is a sacrament implies two things, both equally directly: first, that there is a real sacrifice; second, that it is a sacrifice of a kind unknown to human experience.

It is of utmost importance, in order to safeguard the sacramentality of the sacrifice of Mass, to eliminate from it all such things as would make it into a natural sacrifice, a human act, with human sensations and circumstances. It must be a thing in which the ordinary laws of nature have no part, otherwise it would be, not a sacrament, but a natural event. In order to remain orthodox it is just as necessary to preserve in our minds the sacramentality of the sacrifice of Mass as the real presence of the divine Victim. This attitude I call the negative aspect in the sacramental concept of the sacrifice of Mass.

We take for granted that a sacrifice is the supreme mode of divine worship; we also hold it as certain that the Son of God, dying on the Cross, was a true sacrifice to God. This divine sacrifice, together with all the ritual sacrifices that preceded it and prefigured it under the old dispensation, we have to call natural sacrifices, as they exhibit features which can be observed by our natural powers. Death, which is the most universal element in sacrifice, is easily recognized; the death of Christ on the Cross could be seen by all men: "They shall look on Him whom they have pierced" is Saint John's last phrase in the narration of the Passion. A natural sacrifice is essentially a thing of human observation and experience.

Now the Eucharistic sacrifice is the very opposite; no human experience will tell us the nature of that sacrifice; such a sacrifice is not meant to come under human observation. The sacrifice which is a sacrament belongs to an order of things which could never be known to us except through faith. It is commonly called the mystical sacrifice, or the unbloody sacrifice; but there is no substitute for the one word which alone expresses the matter completely, that it is a sacrament which at the same time is sacrifice, or, better still, that the sacrifice is sacrament. The term "sacramental sacrifice" is no doubt the best, though, for accuracy of language, I would prefer this simple verbal compound—"sacrament-sacrifice."

When, therefore, we meditate on our great sacrifice of the altar, we need not in the least think of any such scene as took place on Calvary; we need not think of the anguish of pain, of any laceration of body; we need not even think of any hypothetical death; in fact, all the things that constitute the natural sacrifice ought to be far removed from our thoughts. My reader will do me the justice of not misunderstanding me here. When assisting at Mass he may meditate on all the terrible and painful circumstances of Christ's historic Passion and Death; there could be no more appropriate subject of contemplation at such a time; what I mean is this, that none of those natural details of Christ's sacrificial act on the Cross are to be read into the sacrament-sacrifice which takes place on the altar.

The Catholic is exhorted over and over again to remember that he is assisting at an unbloody sacrifice; by this expression is meant much more than a mere absence of gruesome circumstance.

The expression signifies a total diversity of the two sacrifices, one being *in natura*, the other being *in sacramento*; this is the greatest difference imaginable. Sacrifice *in sacramento* is not merely an attenuated, a mild form of the natural sacrifice; the two have nothing in common except the divine Victim that is being immolated. We Catholics have that great freedom of mind through our faith in the reality of the Eucharistic sacrifice; we know that through this faith we move in a world which is entirely beyond human experience; we are true mystics, because we hold an infinite reality and yet hold it without any human factors; it is truly the *mysterium fidei*, the mystery of the faith.

We surround the celebration of the Eucharistic sacrifice with every kind of reminder of Christ's real sacrifice on the Cross; we multiply the sign of the Cross over the elements. Mass is a spiritual drama, a mystery play in which we love to re-enact every one of the events that took place between the Garden of Olives and the sepulcher in which Christ's Body was laid; but we know that the sacrament itself, which is being celebrated throughout, has no such human accidents, that it is a simple thing without succession of events; and though it be in our hands, it is still worlds apart from the earthly conditions in which we live.

The Catholic has never found it difficult to see the fitness of Christ's concluding words when He announced the mystery of His Flesh and Blood to be eaten and drunk by man: "The words that I have spoken to you are spirit and life."[73] We find in this utterance the very thing that is dear to us: the profound difference between the natural order and the sacramental order. It is the cherished aim of Christian writers to extol the spiritual, the immaterial, character of the Eucharistic sacrament; and all through Christian literature there flows this double current, the one of faith in the reality of the divine Thing that is contained in the sacrament, and the other of delight in its absolute other-worldliness. The sacramental sphere is an unknown world with a well-known inhabitant.

Could we doubt for one moment the faith of Saint Thomas in the Real Presence? Yet Saint Thomas is one of the most spiritual theologians in this matter of the Eucharist; he is far from being an ultra-realist. In this he resembles Saint Augustine more closely than any modern theologian. Passages like the following, taken from the *Summa*, have a strong Augustinian flavor; yet they never leave the solid ground of the sacramental reality:

> In this sacrament Christ Himself is contained, not indeed in His proper species, but in the species of the sacrament. Therefore it is possible to eat Christ spiritually in a twofold manner; in one way as He exists in His proper species, and in this way the angels eat spiritually Christ Himself, insofar as they are united with Him in the enjoyment of perfect charity and in the clear vision (which sort of bread we also expect to find in heaven), such union not being by faith only, as we have it here on earth.
>
> The other way of eating Christ spiritually is as He is under the appearances of the sacrament, insofar, namely, as a man believes in Christ with a desire of receiving the sacrament; and this is not only eating Christ spiritually, but also eating the sacrament itself, a thing that does not belong to the angels; and therefore, though it behooves the angels to eat Christ spiritually, it does not behoove them to eat the sacrament spiritually.[74]

Let me just add, as a word of comment, that here Saint Thomas does not speak of spiritual communion in the modern sense, but of the worthy sacramental communion which supposes faith and desire. Another golden sentence is to be found in the same Article: "Sacraments are proportioned to faith, through which truth is seen through a glass and in a dark manner, and therefore, properly speaking, it behooves not angels, but men, to eat the sacrament spiritually."[75]

I have already exhorted my readers to rejoice in the truth that sacraments are signs, and not to give up any of the glory of sacramental symbolism, just because Protestantism has distorted the traditional notion of sacramental signification. Let me now urge him to defend against all comers the spiritual character of our sacraments; although again the Protestant Reformers have made of this notion of spirituality an emptying out of the contents of the sacrament. Though the text just cited from Saint Thomas refers more directly to the eating of the bread of the Eucharist, its spirit applies to the Eucharistic sacrifice as well. We are truly dealing with a spiritual sacrifice in the sense that there is no physical death in it, though there be in it all that reality which is indispensable to the sacrifice.

We know the theological grounds on which Protestantism first rejected the notion that in the Eucharist there was a sacrifice besides a communion. If there were a sacrifice, it was objected, it would mean that Christ's sacrifice on the Cross was not complete. The whole answer to this will be given by-and-by; but here we may briefly adumbrate; it does not belong to the nature of the sacrament-sacrifice to supplement, or even to complement, the natural sacrifice. The two sacrifices belong to entirely different spheres or modes of being; one could never, to use a colloquial phrase, stand in the way of the other. Such confusion could only arise in the minds of men unable to see what the sacrament really means. When once we admit that the sacrament-sacrifice has not a vestige of that which constitutes the natural sacrifice, the matter is closed.

In the same order of thought it would be poor theology to make the Eucharistic sacrifice in any way part of Christ's natural sacrifice; to say, for instance, that the Last Supper ought to be considered as the first act in Christ's passion and death. Such a linking up with the natural sacrifice is contrary to the very essence of the sacrament, which could never be an integral part of a natural proceeding. Christ's natural sacrifice and Christ's Eucharistic sacrifice stand to each other in a relationship which is truly unique in the whole realm of revealed truth; one represents the other, but one does not complete the other. The oneness of Christ's redemptive sacrifice is a matter of Catholic dogma; but this oneness is preserved only if we make the distinction, with Saint Thomas, that on Calvary Christ was offered up *in propria specie*, and that on the altar He is offered up *in specie sacramenti*. True oneness is in fact saved only through the total diversity of the two states.

11

The Sacramental View of the Sacrifice of the Mass: Its Positive Aspect

In the preceding chapter we have loosened those bonds with which man's imagination is always tempted to fetter the things of God. Imaginative presentments are not dangerous to faith provided we know their provisional character.

We come now to the real content of that sacrament whose mode of being is so far beyond all known qualifications. How is a sacrament a sacrifice? In answering this question we shall also answer the subsidiary question: "How is the sacrament the food of the soul?" for the Eucharistic food is essentially the banquet that follows the sacrifice. Here more than ever we must cling for our guidance to the all-important principle that we are truly dealing with a sacrament whose very essence it is to be a relationship of signification.

We must approach the question of what is contained in the sacrament through the signs that constitute the sacrament, and not vice versa. It would be quite an erroneous proceeding to say first that the Body and Blood of Christ are contained in the sacrament, and to conclude from this to the sacrifice. Such is not the sacramental proceeding. Our method ought to be quite other. Let us take the signs, both things and words; examine these signs, and see whether they do really signify a sacrifice. If they do signify a sacrifice, then there is a sacrifice, according to the universal axiom that the Christian sacraments do what they signify: *Sacramenta efficiunt quod significant*. This is an extremely important principle, the real crux of sacramental theology. We know the hidden content of the sacrament through the external sign, both things and words, or, to be more technical, its matter and form. The whole power of significance is impressed upon us here.

If God, in His omnipotence, without any human ministry, without any external symbolism, gave grace to the soul of a heathen, this would be an act of mercy, wonderful indeed, but entirely unsacramental. We would know nothing about it, unless we had some special revelation about it. When, on the other hand, a heathen is baptized by another human being, in the Name of the Father and of the Son and of the Holy Spirit, we know what happens in his soul, through the very clear and significant symbolism of that first sacrament.

We learn of the state of the baptized man in the rite of Baptism; we do not discover the significance of the rite through the state of his soul, a thing invisible to us. Baptism, in its traditional sacramental form, is in fact the key that opens our understanding to the excellency of the Christian soul. So in this sacrament of the Eucharist, we know that it is a sacrifice because its words and its elements clearly signify sacrifice; we know that there is the Body and Blood of Christ because the Eucharistic sacrament signifies the Body and Blood of Christ as clearly as Baptism signifies the washing of the soul. Everything else that makes the Eucharist such a marvel of divine power follows upon the signification; it does not precede it. Bread is changed into Christ's Body, wine is changed into Christ's Blood, because the sacramental signification absolutely exacts such a change: for if such a change did not take place the Eucharistic significance would be a false and lying thing.

Saint Thomas expresses this in a few brief words, which we ought to remember at every turn: "The words, through which the consecration takes place, work sacramentally; therefore the power of changing, which is in the forms of these sacraments, follows upon the signification."[76] The meaning of this becomes more clear and informative when we remember the distinction that the Doctor makes between the simple power of God and His sacramental power. God, in this as well as in the other sacraments, works, not through simple omnipotence, but sacramentally; for He gives to the external signs full and complete internal truth and reality, which is a different thing from an absolute act of omnipotence.

"Suppose," says Saint Thomas in so many words, "that God were to say: 'Let this be my Body' in an absolute way, without any historic significance of meaning, as He said at the beginning: 'Let there be light.' Such an act of God would have nothing in common with the Christian sacrament, because, as is evident, the all-important element of significance would be excluded from such an absolute fiat. The Eucharistic sacrament is performed, not through a divine imperative, but through a divine symbolism, or, if you prefer it, through a divine remembrance of the past."

But in justice to the Saint's line of reasoning I must quote the interesting passage in its entirety. To an objector who says that a more suitable formula for the Eucharistic consecration would have been the imperative: "Let this be my Body," as God had commanded, and the heavens and earth were made,

Saint Thomas replies:

> The same word of God which works in the creation of all
> things operates also in this consecration. But in each case in
> a different manner; for here it operates effectively and sacra-
> mentally, i.e., in virtue of its signification. Whence it is fitting
> that the ultimate effect of the consecration be signified by a
> substantive verb in the indicative mood and present tense.
> But in the creation of things it worked simply effectively,
> which efficacy was due to the command of His wisdom, and
> therefore in that creation the divine word is expressed by a
> verb in the imperative mood, according to Genesis 1:3: *Let
> there be light, and light was made.*[77]

These considerations are simply indispensable to any clear
understanding of the Eucharistic mystery. God's omnipotence
in the Eucharist, Saint Thomas insists, is sacramental because it
is in speech and thing, i.e., in the external signification that
His work is accomplished. God's omnipotence does not directly,
immediately, through an imperative fiat, place the Body and
Blood of Christ on the altar; but Christ, the Son of God, first
at the Last Supper, and afterwards through the ministry of His
priests, says certain words and performs certain rites which signify
the sacrifice of His Body and Blood. We must conclude that
there is in that sacramental act the sacrifice of the Body and
Blood of Christ, otherwise the divine signification would be a
falsehood.

But we ought to be more intent on the things Christ actually
does and says at the Last Supper than on the problematic nature
of a hidden thing. Had Christ put His Body and Blood on the
table at the Last Supper absolutely, without any concomitant
element of historical representation, the thing would have
been something totally different from the Christian Eucharist.

The Son of God could, of course, have given to His Church a definite rite, made up of actions and words, of symbols and expressions, which would have been a most telling representation of His sacrifice on the Cross, without such a rite having an inward kernel, so to speak, without its containing the thing it symbolized. The Christian Eucharist has that inward kernel; it is a perfect rite, profoundly significative, for it goes beyond mere signification—it contains what it signifies. Yet, let us say it over and over again, it contains no more than it signifies; for if it did it would not be a sacrament, it would be an absolute act of God's hidden omnipotence, something about which we know nothing. It is perfectly futile in theology to ask questions about the nature of the Eucharistic sacrifice beyond that clearly-marked outline of significance. If in order to explain the nature of the Eucharistic sacrifice we had to fall back upon hidden divine realities not adumbrated by the external signification of the sacrament, we should leave the certain for the uncertain, we should abandon the security of sacramental institutions to go in quest of the unknown.

Let us approach the same subject, so tremendously vital in Catholic thought, from another angle.

Sometimes Catholic apologists of the Real Presence have said that bread and wine are the most unlikely symbols anyone could choose to stand for body and blood. The intention of such well-meaning writers is evident; they are up in arms against Protestant theology, which says that the Eucharist is an excellent symbol of Christ's Body and Blood, but a symbol only. In order to confute the Protestant theologian the incautious apologist denies the significative power of the sacred elements, and thinks that the words of Christ at the institution of the Eucharist must mean the Real Presence because bread and wine could never, even by the widest stretch of imagination, be symbols of body and blood. Who does not see that such defenders deeply compromise Catholic theology? By all means let us protect Catholic doctrine, but not by this method.

Our good friends seem to rejoice in the downright arbitrariness of the divine fiats. But surely we Catholics must defend the sacramental sign with greater tenacity of purpose than anyone else. If the Eucharistic elements were not expressive and symbolic, what would become of the notion of sacrament? The sacrament must signify in words and deeds and things, shall we say to the breaking-point, to the point where it will be necessary, if a lie is to be avoided, that the sacrament should even contain what it signifies. It is as if a man succeeded in acting the part of a king on some mighty stage with such splendor, such wealth, such a number of retainers, such an equipment of military parade, that people would ask themselves the question, where is the difference between this actor-king and the real king? Perhaps hereditary title would be the only thing missing. In the sacrament the Church must act the spiritual thing with such clearness, power and directness, that no one will question her meaning; she really means to accomplish what she acts, as it were, on the stage of sacramental symbolism. The inward reality of the sacrament is the prolongation of the signification of the sacrament. Having gone thus far in saying and doing sacramental things we cannot stop short of the real thing. We all know of the blasphemous gibes of the more ignoble sort of Protestant who uses the hideous word "incantation" to describe the sacramental rites of Catholicism. An incantation is an expression of words and symbols so strong that the very spirits are tied to them. I, for one, shall not blush for the accusation if, in my priestly office, I am supposed to use words and things so expressive that they must have the divine thing irrevocably tied to them. I am not making arbitrary signs and pronouncing words of mere convention when I officiate at the altar and consecrate the bread and wine. I am performing a rite which, if seen in its whole setting, must mean the Body and Blood of Christ as a sweet odor of sacrifice.

Sacramental significance, then, is the only door through which we may draw nigh to the nature of Christ's sacrifice on the altar. We possess what we signify, neither more nor less; if there is more, it is no longer the sacrament; if there is less, we are deceived. The whole question is whether the Eucharistic rite—the words and deeds of Christ first, of ourselves acting in the Person of Christ secondarily—does literally signify Christ's death on the Cross in its reality. The Catholic Church has always maintained that such is the case, and this is why she puts such faith in the sacrifice of the Mass. This book is not written against heretics; it is for the instruction of Catholics, so I do not think it is my duty to defend the Church's position here. My task is to explain to the believer the nature of the sacrifice of the Catholic altar, and the sacrifice is nothing else than the inward kernel of the external, symbolical rite of sacrifice.

The study of the Canon of the Mass is extremely instructive in the light of all that has been said in this chapter. Before and after the essentially sacramental act of consecration, which we may call the major rite of sacrifice, there are many minor sacrificial rites and prayers making that central action more and more expressive, helping it in its work of signification, and leading up gradually from the human to the divine, emphasizing that very thing which I have stated above when I said that the inward thing of the sacrament is the prolongation of the external signification of the sacrament. Let us take the invocation that immediately precedes the solemn moment of consecration: "Do Thou, O God, vouchsafe to make this oblation in all things blessed, approved, ratified, reasonable and acceptable;

that it may become for us the Body and Blood of Thy most beloved Son, our Lord Jesus Christ."[78]

We need not give to the prayers of the Canon, with the exception of the words of consecration, a higher origin than the Church's own inspirations; but they clearly show how the Church understood from the very beginning the great truth that the Eucharistic sacrifice is neither more nor less than the reality signified by the sacramental rite. With such a Faith the Church could supplement the essential signification of the sacrament, which is of divine institution, with her own significations and symbolisms, which are like so many ramifications and radiations of the divine sign. This the Church did for all the other sacraments; the rite of Baptism, for instance, from the very earliest period of Christianity contained acts and symbols which are an evident addition to the baptismal regeneration as enunciated by Christ in the Gospels. The glorious rite of the Mass, developing around the traditional action of the Last Supper, is the most potent instance of that profound instinct of the Catholic Church which tells her that the external sign is the measure and guarantee of the internal reality.

12

The Essence of the Eucharistic Sacrifice

Keenness for divine things and love of objective truth have oftentimes led Catholic divines to the very threshold of the unknown. In this matter of the Eucharistic sacrifice they have tried to find out whether there is, or is not, something that really happens in Christ's own self so as to establish Him in the state of Victim on our altars. The more extreme spirits among them have looked for the essence of the Eucharistic sacrifice in Christ's own self, not in the sacrament. Their craving seems to remain unsatisfied until Christ's own self be directly touched by the knife of immolation. In their controversy with the Protestant symbolists they have become extreme realists, perhaps ultra-realists; and they end by explaining the sacrifice of Mass in terms of Person, no longer in terms of sacrament. It is as if they conceived the process of the Eucharistic sacrifice to be somewhat as follows. The glorious Person of Christ is brought down to the altar through the power of consecration, under the sacramental veil no doubt, yet directly in its totality; and, once made present, it is immolated and offered up as the perfect sacrifice, in some mysterious, indefinable manner. They would call it, perhaps, a sacramental manner, though by a misuse of words; but their commonest term is "mystical." In other words, they put Christ's self first, the sacrifice and the sacrament take second place. This is, I think, a fair description of much theological and devotional phraseology within the liberal tolerance of Catholic dogma.

At first sight it may seem an easier, and even more helpful, concept of the Eucharistic sacrifice, to think of Christ's glorious Person as being in a mysterious way on the altar, as dying mystically, and as being offered up mystically; yet when we come to strict theology, and when we have to state the Eucharist in terms which will make it possible for us to defend it against all enemies, we can no longer express the nature of the Catholic sacrifice in the way just indicated. Need I say that no one need be disturbed if, for the sake of his practical devotion, he adopts the line of thought I have described? The contents of the Eucharistic mystery are so great that whosoever holds faithfully to Transubstantiation and the Real Presence cannot err substantially in his piety. At the same time there is a need for clear thinking in this sublime matter as in everything else, if sentiment, even pious sentiment, is to be kept within the bounds of objective reality.

It is evident that Saint Thomas, who represents so much of Catholic thought and tradition, is far from that view of the Eucharistic sacrifice which I have given above. At no time does he feel the need of asking himself whether anything wonderful happens within Christ's own self when Mass is offered up; in fact it is a cardinal point of his theology to deny any kind of change in Christ's own Person throughout the whole Eucharistic process. Saint Thomas is too keen and clear-headed a sacramentalist ever to become an ultra-realist; even when he says that

Christ is immolated in the sacrament, his whole mode of thinking is sacramental, as his words imply, not natural, in the sense in which in a former chapter we opposed the sacrament to nature.

A long study of the Eucharistic doctrine of Saint Thomas fills one with admiration for his power of grasping a truth and never swerving from it. When one sees how constant has been the tendency of pious men to slip from sacramental thought into natural thought one cannot help but admire the consistency of a theologian who does not betray one single instance of such a lapse.

The essence, then, of the sacrifice of Mass ought to be completely stated before we touch Christ in the personal aspect; that is to say, the Eucharistic sacrifice is not directly a mystery of Christ's Person, it is primarily a mystery of Christ's Body and Blood. Christ's Body is offered up, Christ's Blood is offered up; these are the inward kernel of the external sign in the sacrificial rite; and beyond these—the Body and the Blood—the sacrament, as sacrament, does not go. No conclusion could be more certain. If the Eucharist is to remain a sacrament in our theology, the Body of Christ and the Blood of Christ must be that divine prolongation of our sacramental action at Mass, otherwise the sacrament would not signify the truth. Body and Blood must be the inward kernel of the external signification. In this we must find the whole essence of the sacrifice; I might almost say we must rest content with this and not go beyond, as we have no authority to go further.

When we offer up the great sacrifice we say that we are re-enacting Christ's death sacramentally. Now Christ's death is the separation of His Body and Blood; we do neither more nor less when we sacrifice at the altar. We do not enter directly into the mystery of Christ's Person; we enter into the mystery of His

Body and Blood. Here then we must find the essence of the Eucharistic sacrifice. In the sacrifice of Mass we have the separation of Christ's Body and Blood brought about, not by a fiat of God's omnipotence irrespective of any precedent or human conditions, but as a prolongation of the whole commemorative rite which historically, and as an unbroken chain of remembrance, is linked up with the dead Christ on the Cross.

Absolutely speaking, separation of Body and Blood on the altar would not in itself make a sacrifice, nor would a figurative rite make a true sacrifice; but the two together, one as the human act of commemoration, and the other as the divine prolongation, the inward kernel of reality, of that same act, make the Eucharistic sacrifice. Were we to admit, for the sake of argument, that in the sacrifice of Mass there is some mysterious change in the state of Christ's self, this change could not be anywhere else than in His Body and in His Blood, as the words of consecration do not signify anything sacramentally beyond Body and Blood. It is the Body that is offered up, it is the Blood that is poured out in virtue of the consecration formula. By all the laws of sacramental reality we ought not to look elsewhere in Christ's Person for the essence of the sacrifice than to His Body and Blood, even supposing that an internal change in Christ were necessary in order to make Mass a real and actual sacrifice. But Saint Thomas has succeeded in giving to Mass the highest degree of sacrificial reality, nay, even of immolation, without the necessity of any change whatever in Christ's own self.

It is inevitable that anyone who undertakes to expound these high matters will constantly have to promise further explanations, as he instinctively feels the reader's temporary bewilderment. Here I must promise a chapter on the nature of Eucharistic concomitance, where it will be shown how the whole Person of

Christ, with all the adjuncts of a complete life, may be in the Eucharist, though the precise concept of the Eucharistic sacrifice discards everything except the Body and Blood of Christ.

The Council of Trent insists emphatically on the distinction between the roles of sacrament and of concomitance, copying, almost word for word, the language of Saint Thomas himself. But it is no exaggeration to say that for the purpose of explaining the sacrifice of Mass we need not remember anything else except Christ's Body and Christ's Blood. To such an extent is this true that if Mass had been celebrated by one of the Apostles directly after Christ's death on the Cross, when Body and Blood were separated, and Christ's Soul was in Limbo, there would have been as complete and as true a sacrifice as on any Christian altar today. The principal portion of Christ's human nature, His Soul, would not have been united to that Body and Blood, but this could make no difference in the sacramental sacrifice, for the sacramental signification terminates directly and exclusively in Christ's Body and Christ's Blood. This hypothesis is made much of by Saint Thomas and the other medieval theologians.

> The soul of Christ is in the sacrament through real concomitance, because it is not without the body; but it is not in the sacrament through the power of consecration, and therefore if this sacrament had been consecrated or celebrated at the time when the soul was really separated from the body, the soul of Christ would not have been under the sacrament.[79]

And again:

> If at the time of Christ's passion when the blood was really separated from the body of Christ this sacrament had been consecrated, under the appearance of bread there would have been only the body, and under the appearance of wine there

would have been only the blood."[80]

It is evident from the very nature of the hypothesis here made by Saint Thomas that the reality of the Eucharistic sacrifice could never depend on an intrinsic change, either in Christ's Person or in His Body and Blood, at the moment of the sacrificial immolation on the altar. May we not say that by its very nature the Eucharistic immolation is assumed to take Christ's Body and Blood as it finds them, in the state in which they happen to be? The immolation itself never causes a new state. If Christ, considered in His natural mode of existence, be a mortal man like ourselves, as He was at the Last Supper, the Eucharistic immolation is accomplished in the mortal Body and Blood; if Christ be in the glorious state, as He is now in heaven, the Eucharistic immolation is accomplished in an immortal Body and Blood; if Christ be actually dead, the Eucharistic immolation is accomplished in a Body and Blood which are not quickened by the Soul. In other words, the Eucharistic immolation transcends the states either of Christ's Person or of His Body and Blood; it does not cause any state. Such varieties of state are caused by Christ's natural mode of existence, at the time. This projection, as we might call it, of either the transient or the permanent state of Christ into the Eucharistic existence is thus stated by Saint Thomas:

> Whatever belongs to Christ as He is in Himself, may be attributed to Him both in His natural existence and in His sacramental existence, such as to live, to die, to suffer pain, to be animate or inanimate, and other such attributes. But whatever concerns Christ in connection with external bodies, can be attributed to Him in His natural existence only, and not in His sacramental existence, such as to be mocked, to be spat upon, to be crucified, to be scourged, and other such things.[81]

The meaning of Saint Thomas is clear and extremely important. Diversity of state in the sacrament comes only from the diverse modes of Christ's natural existence; sacramental immolation, as such, does not cause a new kind of state. Assuming an even bolder hypothesis, Saint Thomas maintains that if an Apostle had consecrated at the actual moment of Christ's dying, or if the consecrated elements had been preserved during the whole drama of Christ's agony on the Cross, there would have been real suffering and real death in the blessed sacrament then, though there would not have been in the sacrament the external violence done to Christ's Body by the executioners. "And therefore Christ as He is under the sacrament cannot suffer [external violence], but He can die."[82] Suppositions like these are very instructive because they bring home to us the great truth that if there are changes in Christ's state under the Eucharistic form, such changes are not the result of the sacramental immolation, but they are anterior to it; we offer up at the altar the Body and Blood such as we find them.

There is undoubtedly a tendency in modern piety to read into the mystery of the Eucharistic sacrifice certain factors of a more extreme kind which seem to give greater reality to the Eucharistic immolation than is warranted by the strictly sacramental view. But let us constantly remember that in the sacrament we are not dealing with the natural life of Christ; we are dealing with His representative life. The Eucharistic Body and Blood represent Christ's natural Body and Blood. The Protestant would go only so far as to say that the Eucharistic bread and wine represent Christ's Body and Blood; the Catholic goes beyond that and says that Christ's Body under the appearance of bread and Christ's Blood under the appearance of wine represent His natural Body and Blood as they were on Calvary. This is the true and final expression of sacramental representation; and such representation suffices by itself to constitute the sacrifice, because the representation is of that moment of Christ's wonderful existence when He was truly the Victim of sacrifice, His precious Blood drained from His Body.

Protestantism has denied the Eucharistic sacrifice on various grounds, into which we need not enter now. The non-Catholic frame of mind which in a way is nearest to Catholicism is that which admits all, or nearly all, of the Catholic doctrine of the Real Presence, and yet denies the Eucharistic sacrifice. The earlier periods of Protestantism, chiefly of Lutheranism, exhibited that attitude of an almost total faith in the Eucharistic realities combined with fierce denial of the Eucharistic sacrifice. To meet this kind of unbelief the Church might have adopted two lines of defense. First she might have said that the whole Eucharistic doctrine, as it stands, as the Scriptures reveal it, as those very Protestants of the less aggressive type hold it, with the dual consecration, must be a sacrifice if it has any meaning at all; that the Church, in her Eucharistic liturgy as handed down from the Apostles, is a sacrificant as well as a communicant, from the very nature of the case. On the other hand the Church might have appealed to another revelation claiming a traditional consciousness of a hidden element of sacrifice which is not evident in the Eucharistic rite itself, but which is known to the Church in virtue of an *ad hoc* revelation. The Church would then have made it her business to produce the authentic proofs of such revelation.

Now we know that the Church has chosen the former of the two alternatives. She has maintained that the Eucharistic rite, learned from Christ and His Apostles, with the dual consecration and all the sacramental signification that surrounds it, is a true sacrifice. The Church does not appeal to a hidden element, to something recondite, not plainly manifested in the Eucharistic revelation contained in the Scriptures. The Church says this: the Eucharist as we have learned it from the Son of God and His Apostles, as even those well-meaning Protestants hold it, is an evident sacrifice in the eyes of all those who have the clear vision of the things of Christ.

13

Eucharistic Representation, Application, and Immolation

In the Eucharistic mystery Body and Blood exist separately—through a sacramental separation completely sufficient for the purpose—though the natural Person of Christ be whole and entire.

Christ, who gave His Body and Blood to the Apostles at the Last Supper, was whole and entire at the head of the festive board. The Christ whose Body and Blood is on the Catholic altar is whole and entire in heaven. But the Eucharistic Body and Blood are representations of Christ in the state in which He was not whole and entire; when He was broken on the Cross at His death. The Eucharistic Body and Blood at the Last Supper, therefore, were the representation, or more accurately the presentation, of the Christ who would be broken on the Cross the following day, not of the Christ who was there at the head of the table. The Eucharistic Body and Blood on our altars are the re-presentation—here the word (taken in its radical meaning) is quite accurate—not of the Christ who is in heaven, but again of the Christ who was broken on Calvary.

If we were to say that at the sacrifice of Mass Christ comes

down from heaven and is sacrificed again, we should be express-
ing the mystery of the Eucharist in a totally wrong way. Such
phrases, of course, may be allowed in ordinary devotional
language; but they would be quite inaccurate theologically. If
by some supposition Christ were to come down from heaven
in Person, and if He were sacrificed on the altar, such an event
would be something quite different from the Eucharistic sacrifice. It is the very nature of the Eucharistic sacrifice to be a
representation of the past, not a mactation in the present.
Christ's Body and Blood represent aptly and completely that
phase of His earthly career when He was dead on the Cross;
they do not represent in any way that other phase of Christ's
existence, His glorious life in heaven. The full Person of Christ
brought down on our altars could not at the same time be a
representation of Himself. The mere memory of the death of
Christ could never be the living Lord; but His Body and Blood,
separated in sacramental truth, can be the memory or representation of that Lord whose Body was on the Cross, whose Blood
was poured out on the hill of Calvary.

The Eucharistic sacrifice, then, is essentially representative;
it puts on the altar the Christ of Calvary, the same that Mary
beheld as she gazed at the Body of her dead Son hanging on the
Cross. We have already said that each one of the seven sacraments
is representative of the passion of Christ in its own way; but
the Eucharist represents it in a most realistic fashion, because it
is what Christ was at one time, Body and Blood. When Christ
was Body and Blood only He was the perfect sacrifice; and the
Eucharist is a perfect sacrifice because it again makes present—
such is the literal meaning of re-presentation—all there was on
this earth of Christ after He had pronounced His *consum-
matum est* (it is finished), when His Soul had been given up to
the Father.

We have, therefore, in the Eucharist two degrees of signification which are interdependent and complementary to each other. To have this additional degree of signification and representation of Christ's death makes the Eucharist the supreme sacrament. Let us remember what we have said of the distinction between "sacrament" on the one hand, and "sacrament and thing" on the other.[83] In the Eucharist the "sacrament and thing" are the Body and Blood of Christ. Not only does the Eucharist have the power of signification as "sacrament only," but also as "sacrament and thing," for the Body and the Blood of Christ in the Eucharist are representative—that is, they signify in absolute literalness Christ as He hung on the Cross.

Though we insist so much on the truth that at the consecration in the Mass we come into contact directly, in virtue of the sacrament, with Christ's Body and Blood, not with His whole Person, the representation, which is the very nature of the Eucharistic sacrifice, terminates in that sacred Person; but the Person broken on Calvary, not the whole Person of the Last Supper or of heaven. That Christ should have ever been one who was Body and Blood in a state of separation gives to the Eucharistic separation of Body and Blood its whole meaning. The Eucharistic separation of Body and Blood is the memory, the representation, of that real separation in historic time. Body and Blood separated upon the altar would have no meaning but for the historic precedent on Calvary when the last drop of Christ's Blood was drained from His Body. The Eucharistic representation is indeed something in which metaphors have no place; it is a thing of absolute literalness.

By application we mean that individual benefit to every believer in Christ's passion; the merit, the sacrificial atonement of that great immolation on the Cross coming down on the individual man and entering his soul. The Eucharistic sacrifice is the divine means whereby the individual believer comes into contact with the sacrifice of the Cross.

Here, again, I must be allowed to make a promise of a more ample treatment of this matter later on. At present I am concerned with the relationship of the Eucharistic Body and Blood with the Christ on the Cross. As the Body and Blood on the altar are such a perfect representation of the broken Son of God on Calvary, they are also the most immediate and complete contact of the soul with all the saving power of Golgotha. So it can be said that in the Eucharistic sacrifice Christ is truly immolated, because the immolation of Christ on Calvary is brought home to us in such a realistic manner. We do not say that Christ is immolated anew in the Eucharistic sacrifice, for this would mean a substantial process of disintegration in the very Person of Christ such as He is now, a thing not to be admitted. But we do say that He is immolated, because the Calvary immolation is represented so truly, and is applied so directly, through the Eucharistic Body and Blood. It would not be enough, in order to explain the total range of the Eucharistic sacrifice, to say that at the altar we offer up the Body and Blood of Christ; we do more, we immolate Christ, but—and here is an immense difference—not the Christ who is in heaven, because as such He is not represented on the altar at all, but the Christ of Calvary, as the Christ of Calvary is the only one who is represented on the altar.

The one great truth that illumines the Eucharistic doctrine with a light as clear as that of the rising sun is that one phase of the career of the Son of God on earth is kept perpetually present amongst us with an exactness of reproduction that is truly astonishing. After His death, and before His Resurrection, Christ was truly on this earth; but in what a state! His Body was lifeless and bloodless, His Blood was poured out, and the earth drank it as it had drunk the blood of Abel; yet in this broken condition the Person of Christ remained, for the death of Christ was not as the death of Abel. Hypostatic Union survived that great dissolution—that is to say, the divine Person of the Word remained united as before, both with the Body and the Blood of Christ; the Person of Christ as Person remained entire, though His human nature had been broken; so that it may be said in all exactness of theological language, that the Body and the Blood on Calvary or in the sepulcher were Christ, on account of the divine Person hypostatically united to them. The Son of God never ceased to be a complete Person, even in death, a thing which is not to be admitted of the human dead, who cease to be persons in the real sense of the word.

This aspect of the Incarnation is so important and of such relevance to the Eucharistic mystery that I do not hesitate to enter into it more fully and to quote from an earlier portion of the Third Part of the *Summa*, where Saint Thomas treats of Christ's descent into limbo. The Third Article of Question Fifty-Two asks: "Whether the whole Christ was in Limbo?" He begins by quoting Saint Augustine: "The whole Son is with the Father; He is whole in heaven, whole on earth, whole in the womb of the Virgin, whole on the Cross, whole in Hades, whole in Paradise, whither He ushered in the thief."[84] Then he gives his own explanation:

> Though in death the soul of Christ was separated from His body, neither soul nor body were separated from the Person of the Son of God ... therefore we must confess that in that triduum of His death the whole Christ was in the sepulcher, because the whole Person was there as having that body united to Itself; and likewise the whole Christ was in Limbo, because the whole Person of Christ was there by reason of the soul united to Itself; moreover, the whole Christ was then

everywhere by reason of the divine nature.[85]

Two precious sentences from Saint Thomas's replies to objectors throw additional light on this matter.

> The fact that the body of Christ was not in Limbo does not exclude the fact of the whole Christ being in Limbo; but it only means this, that in Limbo there was not the whole of that which belongs to the human nature.
>
> Through the oneness of soul and body the totality of the human nature is constituted, but not the totality of the divine Person; and therefore after the separation of soul and body through death the whole Christ remained, but His human nature did not remain in its wholeness.[86]

Let us be quite assured that nothing is more orthodox than to speak of the dead Christ in the full amplitude of complete Personality.

We may, then, consider Christ's Person in three phases: His mortality, from the moment of His birth to His death on the Cross; His immortality, from the Resurrection *in saecula saeculorum* (forever and ever); in between comes His death, which lasted but a short time, yet which, in spite of that great severance between Body and Soul, between Flesh and Blood, is one of the three periods under which the Person of Christ is known to our faith. I do not crave my reader's forgiveness for bringing into play here some of the principles of the Hypostatic Union. Could we ever expect to understand the Eucharist without its ramifications into the larger and profounder mystery of the union between a divine Person and His human nature? But who does not see how the Eucharist becomes a thing of palpitating reality if it is made clear that the one phase of the Christ-career which is the most sublime and the most heroic—His state of immolation as the divine Victim—is brought back to us in the identical elements that constituted it nearly two thousand years ago: Body on the one hand and Blood on the other hand, hypostatically united with the divine Person?

This and nothing less is meant by that representation which holds such a place in the traditional Eucharistic doctrine; this and nothing less is implied by that application to the individual soul of Christ's death on Calvary. All the treasures of Calvary, Body and Blood, clothed in divine Personality, are poured into our bosom; this and nothing less is the meaning of that immolation of Christ which Catholic tradition maintains as belonging to the Eucharistic sacrifice.

If the dead Christ on Calvary is a Victim that is immolated, then of course by sheer equation of truth Christ is immolated on our altar; because the same Christ, that Christ of the second phase who was on Calvary, is on the altar in absolute identity. We think neither of the Christ of the first phase nor of the Christ of the third phase when we speak of the immolated Christ; we think of the Christ of the middle phase. Here indeed is the *Christus passus*—the Christ who has suffered—who is thus contained in the Eucharist. In virtue of the sacrament, the Eucharist contains, not the mortal Christ, nor even the dying Christ, nor does it contain the glorious Christ; but it contains the Christ directly after His death. "For as often as you shall eat this bread and drink the chalice, you shall show the death of the Lord, until He come."[87]

From this we see that a very important distinction is necessary when we speak of Christ as contained in the Eucharist. At the Last Supper, when the mortal Christ celebrated the Eucharistic mystery, in virtue of His direct act He was contained in the Eucharist in that phase of His existence which was to come about soon after on Calvary; but in virtue of concomitance He was contained therein in the fullness of the mortal phase of His divine Personality. If Mass had been celebrated during the three days of Christ's death the Eucharist would have contained the second phase of the Christ-personality, and nothing more; there would have been no other concomitant personal quality. Today on our altar, in virtue of the sacrament we have that second or middle phase of the Christ-personality; but in virtue of concomitance we have also the whole third phase in the Christ-personality, His glorious life. But when treating of the sacrifice we need not think of any other presentation except that of the second phase of the Christ-personality.

Such, then, is the content of the Eucharistic sacrament. Christ in the state of Victim before God, His Body and Blood a sacrifice of sweet savor to the Lord. "This is the difference between the Eucharist and the other sacraments which have an external matter, that the Eucharist contains a sacred thing absolutely, that is to say, Christ Himself."[88] "The Eucharist is the sacrament of the passion of Christ, inasmuch as man is rendered perfect by being linked up with the dead Christ."[89]

Once more let me remind the reader that in a later chapter we shall enter more fully into the nature of the sacrifice of the Cross, and there it will be shown more clearly how Christ's sacrifice on the Cross was essentially a thing of Body and Blood. But I trust that I have made it clear in this chapter how we may, on the one hand, make of the sacramental Body and Blood of Christ the basis of all our study of the Eucharist, and how, on the other hand, we come, through those divine elements, into direct and sacramental contact with the Person of Christ, I mean with the *Christus passus* of Calvary, represented, applied, immolated, and contained in the Eucharistic sacrifice.

14

The Oneness of the Christian Sacrifice

It is well known that the most constant reproach of Protestantism against the Catholic doctrine of the Eucharistic sacrifice is this, that the Catholic Church, by teaching the need of a second sacrifice, virtually denies the all-sufficiency of the sacrifice on Calvary. Yet the Church has never ceased protesting that her Eucharistic sacrifice is by no means a derogation of the natural sacrifice of Christ on the Cross; it is, on the contrary, an additional honor to that great act by which Christ redeemed us. The sacrifice of the Christian altar and the Sacrifice of Calvary are one and the same. At the same time the Church maintains that the Mass is a sacrifice in the true sense of the word, an act which is new every day, though the sacrifice be not new. We have, then, in this matter unity and duality of a very peculiar nature. It is my conviction that unless we cling firmly to the sacramental concept of the Eucharistic sacrifice we cannot meet the Protestant difficulty. But if once we grasp the meaning of the sacrament, the Protestant difficulty vanishes, and the fundamental oneness of the Christian sacrifice becomes apparent.

If the Eucharistic sacrifice were in any way a natural sacrifice it would be simply impossible to avoid the conclusion that there are two different sacrifices, and the question: Why two sacrifices? would be justifiable. The circumstance that the second sacrifice would take place under entirely different conditions would not save us from such a conclusion; if it were a sacrifice *in natura*, however much disguised, it would be really another sacrifice, not the same sacrifice. But let the sacrifice be a sacrament in the full sense of the word, then it cannot be a new sacrifice, but it must be the representation, pure and simple, of the historic or natural sacrifice. If there were in the Mass an immolation, or a mactation, or a death, or an heroic deed, not already contained in the sacrifice of the Cross, the Eucharist would at once become sacrifice number two, because in that case something new would have happened in the world of grace which did not happen on the Cross.

It is the genius and very nature of the Christian sacrament to be an act which may be repeated indefinitely, though the content, or, if you like, the object of the act, be immutable. This is the representative role of the Christian sacrament. Such a thing cannot happen anywhere outside the sacramental sphere. Is not the sacrament precisely this mystery of never ceasing repetition or representation of something in itself immutable? If Christ came to us in His natural state and were thus offered up, this new coming and this new offering would be events forming new chapters in the historic career of the Son of God. But the sacramental presence and the sacramental offering of Christ are not historic events in His career; they do not form new chapters in the book of His life. Of course, the acts by which He instituted the Eucharist and offered Himself up for the first time are most tremendous deeds in His historic career; but to be offered up in the sacrament does not belong to the historic life of the Son of God. If there is repetition of acts, those repetitions are not on the part of Christ, they are on the part of the Church living here on earth. "As the thing which is offered up everywhere is one Body and not many bodies, so there is one sacrifice everywhere."[90]

It is such a pity to see how often an initial misconception in these high matters leads to profound divergences of thought, nay, even to dangerous presentments of Catholic truth. To save the oneness of the Christian sacrifice the strange hypothesis has been put forward in our own days that the Eucharistic sacrifice is not so much a representation of the sacrifice of the Cross as an integral portion of the sacrifice of the Cross. The Eucharistic sacrifices, both at the Last Supper and now, are being considered as so many stages in the one great all-embracing sacrifice whose culminating act was on the Cross.

It is not my mission here to criticize theological opinions. It is certain, however, that to consider the Eucharistic sacrifice as being in any way a portion of the universal sacrifice is a profound reversal of the traditional role of the sacrament. A sacrament is not an act in the drama, however great that drama may be; a sacrament is essentially the representation of the whole drama. The historic drama must be complete before sacraments are possible. Sacraments are the monuments of the finished thing, not the introductory scenes or the last acts of some great historic deed. If the Eucharistic sacrifice were in any way a portion of the universal sacrifice it would represent nothing except itself; it would contain nothing except itself; it would not apply to us anything except such grace as would belong to it in its partial role; it would not contain more immolation than would be warranted by its essentially limited place in a greater mystery. Now the Christian sacrament, and above all, the sacrament-sacrifice, is a representation, an application, an immolation, and a containing of the whole immensity of the universal sacrifice. We must, if we are to save the dignity of the Catholic Mass, make it a thing by itself, not merely the first or last act of another thing, however divine and powerful.

I can understand the temptation that comes to anyone who lets go his grasp of the sacramental view in general, and more particularly of the sacramental view of the Eucharistic sacrifice. He finds himself confronted with an awkward duality, which he hopes to reconcile by making Mass a part of the Christian sacrifice. He thus invokes what might be called a oneness of organism, as when we call "one" the various members of the same body. In the theory I allude to, Mass is only a member, it is not the whole thing. But in the traditional view Mass is the whole thing; it contains the whole Christ with the kind of totality described in the last chapter. Is not one of the basic principles of the Eucharistic sacrifice to be found in the very completeness and finality of the sacrifice of the Cross? If Mass gave anything to the Cross it would cease to be a sacrament, as it would cease to be a representation. Mass is the memory or the monument of Christ's passion. Is it not the very purpose of a monument to stand for the complete victory, the final triumph? We do not erect monuments to deeds incomplete or half-achieved, however heroic they may be. To take away something from the completeness of the sacrifice of the Cross on the one hand, and on the other hand from the completeness of the sacrifice of the Mass, is not to join them into one organism; it is to maim them both. In this matter you cannot make a whole with two halves, because sacrament and nature are totally different. But they become one through that very difference, as I have already said, because the one is the total representation of the other's totality of reality. The traditional view of the Church, as I shall prove by-and-by, is that the sacrifice of Calvary was complete and perfect of its kind; the Eucharist adds nothing to it, but it is truly "the brightness of its glory and the figure of its substance."

To come back to the Protestant, we may say to him that his position is in a way comprehensible if he denies the whole sacramental system, root and branch, making of faith alone his approach to Christ; but if a man admits sacraments at all there is no more reason for him to reject the sacrament-sacrifice than to reject the sacrament-regeneration—i.e., Baptism. In both we have nothing else than a representation—in the technical sense of the word—of Christ's death and its application to the individual soul. If Baptism is no derogation to Christ's sacrifice on Calvary, but is, on the contrary, the sign of Christ's victory, why should the Eucharistic sacrifice be such a derogation? Are we not dealing in both instances with modes of contact between the individual soul and the historic Christ? The Eucharistic sacrifice may be a more vivid representation, or, if you like, a more burning contact, having more of activity than of passivity, containing a divine substance; but when all is said there is no radical difference in strict theological thought between Baptism and the Eucharist, considered in its true sacramental functions of sacrifice and spiritual nutriment.

This seems a fitting place for the examination of a difficulty which may sometimes bewilder even careful thinkers in theological matters. The Eucharistic sacrifice was offered up first at the Last Supper, before the natural sacrifice on the Cross took place. Would not this point to the conclusion that in some way the Eucharistic sacrifice is truly the beginning of the whole sacrificial drama of Christ? Did He not, when He offered Himself in sacrifice in the supper room, perform the first act of that priesthood which reached its consummation on Calvary? Here, again, one must admit that it would be difficult, not to say impossible, to fit the Last Supper into the act of redemption if we gave to the Eucharistic sacrifice the meaning and the value of a natural sacrifice. If it were a natural sacrifice, we could not avoid the conclusion that the world was redeemed before Christ shed His first drop of Blood, as the Last Supper would have had infinite value as sacrifice in its own right.

The other alternative would be, of course, the one adopted by some recent theologians whose views have already been mentioned, who consider the Last Supper to have been merely the first act of the one universal sacrifice, and who make the sacramental reality and the natural reality complement each other. But if once the sacramental view of the Eucharistic sacrifice is admitted, the difficulty no longer exists. As the sacrament is essentially a representation, it could be instituted at any moment by Christ, provided He existed bodily in the reality of the Incarnation, and not only in the hope of the believer. That great act of Redemption, the immolation of Christ on the Cross, could be represented before, as well as after, His crucifixion; and though the sacrament derives all its truth and value from the death of Christ, its institution, or even its celebration or use, may precede that event. The celebration of the Eucharistic sacrifice by Christ no more superseded His role on Calvary than did the first breaking of bread of the Christian Church after the coming of the Holy Spirit. Sacraments, and sacraments only, possess that aloofness from the historical sequence of events.

Speaking of Baptism, Saint Thomas gives us in very succinct phrases the theology of those wonderful anticipations by Christ. Taking it for granted that men may have received Christian Baptism before Christ died on the Cross, he says: "Even before Christ's passion Baptism received its efficacy from Christ's passion, as it was its figure; but it prefigured differently from the sacraments of the Old Law, as these were mere figures;

but Baptism derived the power of justifying from that very Christ by whose virtue the passion itself was to become salutary."[91]

Applying this doctrine to the Eucharistic sacrifice of the Last Supper, we may say that it prefigured the sacrifice of the Cross; and the Christ who was to give His own natural Flesh and Blood that power of redeeming mankind, gave to bread and wine the power of representing sacramentally that same Flesh and Blood. We need not even consider the Eucharistic sacrifice of the Last Supper as being a final vow of the Son of God to undergo death, a theme beloved of more than one preacher. The traditional view of the Last Supper is much more sacramental in tenor: Christ, on the eve of leaving this world, gave us the memory or monument of Himself, and nothing in the nature of that great monument obliged Christ to wait until after the event for this. The monument is such that He could erect it before the event, it being a sacrament. The institution of the Eucharistic sacrament at the Last Supper, then, was not so much Christ's vow to die, as His anticipated triumph in His death.

15

Saint Thomas and the Council of Trent on the Oneness of the Christian Sacrifice

If it is a commonplace in the history of religious thought that no error ever achieves success except through the truth on which it feeds, at no time was this more evident than when the Reformers started preaching the uselessness of the Eucharistic Sacrifice. Indeed their success came from the most permanent of Christian truths, the all-sufficiency of the Sacrifice of the Cross. Hence it became imperative in the Catholic counter-reformation to examine more deeply the relationship between the Sacrifice of the Cross and the Eucharistic Sacrifice. The results of that great labor of investigation and restatement are embodied in the First and Second Chapters of the Twenty-Second Session of the Council of Trent. The remarkable feature, however, of that most scholarly and exact presentment of the Catholic doctrine of the Eucharistic sacrifice by the Fathers of Trent is this, that it gives an exact reproduction of the doctrine of Saint Thomas, whose line of thought and whose very expressions are easily recognized in its more classical treatment of the subject.

One very important Article of the *Summa* is obviously embodied in the conciliar pronouncement, namely the First Article of the Eighty-Third Question: "Whether Christ be immolated in this sacrament?" I shall first give the text of Saint Thomas with a few comments, and then the words of the Council. Taken in conjunction, the two authorities, so separate in time, will make it clear to us how the Eucharist is a sacrifice, and is one and the same sacrifice with that of the Cross.

> The celebration of this sacrament is called an immolation of Christ for a twofold reason. Firstly, because, as Augustine says in his letter to Simplicianus: "the images of things are called by the names of those things which they represent; so that if we look at a picture we say: This is Cicero and that is Sallust." But the celebration of this sacrament ... is an image representing Christ's Passion, which is His true immolation; therefore, the celebration of this sacrament is called Christ's immolation....
>
> Secondly, it is called an immolation of Christ in respect of the effect of His Passion, since it is through this sacrament that we are made partakers of the fruits of the Lord's Passion, as we declare in one of the Sunday Secrets (Ninth after Pentecost): "As often as the commemoration of this sacrifice is celebrated the work of our Redemption is accomplished."
>
> As far as the first mode is concerned then it is true to say that Christ was immolated, even in the figures of the Old Testament; hence the words of Revelation, chapter 13: "Whose names are not written in the Book of Life of the Lamb, which was slain from the beginning of the world." But according to the second mode, it is proper to this sacrament that in its celebration Christ is immolated. (*Sed quantum ad secundum modum, proprium est huic sacramento, quod in ejus celebratione Christus immoletur.*)[92]

I quote the Latin of the last sentence because a certain amount of misunderstanding has surrounded this text. It is evident, after a careful perusal of the words of Saint Thomas, that he makes immolation in the Eucharist conterminous with representation and application. He makes a distinction, however, between representation and application, because application could only belong to the sacrament of the New Law, while representation may be predicated also of the sacraments of the Old Law, though, of course, in a much more shadowy manner. The sacrament of the Old Law could never share in that thing which is called sacramental application; this is proper and exclusive to the sacrament of the New Law. Saint Thomas here repeats the doctrine enunciated in a previous Article[93]—namely, that the death of Christ being the efficient cause of salvation, it could not be applied to us except through the very fact of Christ having existed and having died in reality; a mere hope of a coming Christ could not be an efficient cause applicable to the soul through real contact. Saint Thomas does not make a distinction between representation and application to the extent of causing a difference in the concept of Eucharistic immolation; all he means to say is this, that the kind of immolation which is conterminous with application could never be found outside the sacrament of the New Law, while the immolation, which is conterminous with representation, may be found, at least in a shadowy way, in the Jewish rites. In the sacrament of the Eucharist, then, representation and application of the sacrifice of the Cross are the only kind of immolation to be admitted in the sacrifice of the Christian altar. The Cross is Christ's true immolation; the Mass is its perfect image, therefore it is an immolation.[94]

Saint Thomas was well aware of those very objections which a few centuries later became such terrific issues. Is it not strange how at one period men formulate objections and their faith is not impaired, while at another time the same difficulties, in no wise more acute, become battle-cries of a spiritual revolution? The first of these runs as follows:

> It would seem that in the celebration of this sacrament Christ is not immolated, for it is said in the tenth chapter of Hebrews that Christ *by one oblation has perfected forever them that are sanctified.* Now such an oblation was His immolation. Christ, therefore, is not immolated in the celebration of this sacrament.

Protestantism has not formulated anything more definite against the Eucharistic sacrifice. Let us hear the answer.

> Saint Ambrose says: "One is the victim" which indeed Christ offered and which we offer, "and the victims are not many, because Christ was offered up but once." Now this sacrifice is exemplary of that other. For as that which is offered up everywhere is one body and not many bodies, so also there is but one sacrifice.

Here Saint Thomas gives the intrinsic and final reason to the oneness of the Christian sacrifice. The Body which is offered up is one and the same everywhere, be it on the Cross, be it on the Christian altar. The sacrifice of Calvary and the sacrifice of the Eucharist are to each other in the relationship of pattern and replica; the one contains exactly what the other contains.

A second objection runs:

> The immolation of Christ was accomplished on the Cross on which *He delivered Himself an oblation and a sacrifice to God for an odor of sweetness,* as is said in the fifth chapter of Ephesians; but in the celebration of this mystery Christ is not crucified, therefore He is not immolated.

The answer of Saint Thomas shows how very little he was prepared to admit any kind of realistic crucifixion or the like in the Eucharistic sacrifice. "As the celebration of this sacrament is the representative image of the passion of Christ, so is the altar representative of the Cross itself on which Christ was immolated in His own nature." Here again representation is the link between Cross and altar.

The third difficulty goes one step further. Quoting Saint Augustine the objector says that in the immolation of Christ the priest and the victim are the same; but in the celebration of this sacrament the priest and the victim are not the same; therefore the celebration of the sacrament could never be an immolation of Christ. Now for the answer. "In the same line of thought the priest also is the image of Christ, in whose Person and by whose power he pronounces the words of consecration ... and so in that way the priest and the victim are the same."

This carries the representative character of the Eucharistic immolation to the utmost degree of reality. In the Eucharist we have that which made even Christ's natural immolation so remarkable, that the priest and the victim were the same. We see here how Saint Thomas differs in a way from more modern presentments of the same subject. For him there are two representative elements, the priest at the altar and the sacramental Body and Blood. The priest represents Christ; the Eucharistic elements represent Christ's Body and Blood. The more modern way differs from this; it says that Christ Himself in His own Person is the priest who officiates at the altar as He officiated on Calvary. But surely the way of Saint Thomas is more in keeping with the whole sacramental doctrine, for the Christian priesthood is as truly representative of Christ's priesthood as the Eucharistic Body is representative of Christ's natural Body.

The Christian priesthood is as truly a sacrament as the Christian sacrifice is a sacrament. The two stand to each other in the relation in which Christ stood to His immolation on the Cross. Sacramentally the Catholic priesthood is one with the Eucharistic victim as naturally Christ was one with that which He offered on the Cross. But of this more will be said later.

Let us now come to the text of the Council of Trent. We are dealing with a Latin style very different from the simple and direct phraseology of Saint Thomas; yet the ideas and many of the expressions of the Angelic Doctor are to be found quite undisguised in the Tridentine decrees. We must, however, split up the phrases of the Renaissance Latin into their constituent parts with a certain amount of liberty, for the diction is intricate far beyond our modern directness of style. On the whole, in our everyday speech we resemble Saint Thomas more closely than the sixteenth century divines.

Our God and Lord [Jesus Christ] although about to offer Himself to God the Father once through His death upon the Altar of the Cross for an eternal redemption, yet at the Last Supper, on the night that He was betrayed, offered up His Body and Blood under the appearance of bread and wine. This He did that His death might not put an end to His priesthood, and that He might give to His beloved Bride, the Church, a visible sacrifice in keeping with the needs of man's nature. Through this the bloody sacrifice about to be accomplished on the Cross would be represented, its memory would endure to the end of the world, and its saving power be applied for the remission of our daily sins. Thus He declared Himself *a priest forever ever according to the order of Melchizedek.*[95] Under these same symbols He gave His Body and Blood to His Apostles to eat and drink; and gave to them and their successors a command to offer a like sacrifice: *Do this in commemoration of Me,*[96] and thus He ordained them priests of the New Testament. This is what the Catholic Church has always understood and taught. After celebrating that ancient Pasch, which the multitudes of the Children of Israel were wont to immolate in memory of their escape from Egypt, Christ instituted the New Pasch, His very Self to be immolated under visible signs by the Church, through the ministry of her priests, in memory of His passage from this world to His Father, whereby through the pouring out of His Blood He redeemed us, *delivered us from the power of darkness, and hath translated us into His Kingdom....*[97]

And since in this divine Sacrifice, which is celebrated at Mass, that same Christ is contained and immolated in an unbloody manner, who once on the Altar of the Cross offered Himself through the shedding of His Blood, it is the teaching of this holy Synod that the sacrifice [of the Mass] is truly a sacrifice of propitiation, through which, provided we approach it with right intention and faith, with fear and reverence, *we shall obtain mercy and find grace in seasonable aid.*[98] Appeased by the oblation of this sacrifice the Lord, bestowing the grace and gift of penance, forgives even the most heinous crimes and sins. For the Victim is one and the same; He who then offered Himself on the Cross now offers Himself through the ministry of His priests, only in the manner of offering is there any difference. Of that offering [through bloodshed] the fruits come to us most abundantly through this unbloody sacrifice. Nothing, then, is further [from the mind of the Church] than that the latter should in the least way derogate from the former. Wherefore this [Sacrifice of the Altar] is rightly offered, according to Apostolic tradition, not only for the sins, guilt and satisfactions, of the faithful on earth, but, even for those who have died in Christ.[99]

We have in these decrees concerning the Eucharistic Sacrifice words enough on which to ring the changes: representation, application, immolation, memory, and containing. The Fathers of the Council accept the same duality as Saint Thomas: the sacrifice of the Cross is an absolutely complete act, and the sacrifice of the Altar is equally a complete act. Oneness of Christian sacrifice is found in perfect representation, application, and containing.

I do not press further comparison between the conciliar formula and the Article of Saint Thomas, on which we have already commented in this chapter; the resemblances are too obvious to need emphasis. Let me only remark that the Council makes it quite clear that the Last Supper was a complete act, representing in anticipation that other complete act, the sacrifice of the first Good Friday. There is not a hint in Tridentine theology of those recent theories which make the Last Supper part of the whole sacrifice; in fact, one wonders how, in the face of such clear pronouncements, anyone could be so bold as to disturb the traditional order of the redemptive dispensation—i.e., first the institution of the commemorative sacrifice; second, the natural sacrifice; third, the celebration, no longer by Christ, but by the priest, of the commemorative sacrifice. The Council of Trent safeguards the oneness of the Calvary sacrifice and the Eucharistic sacrifice precisely because it keeps them so well apart in their respective modes of being.

"The sacrifice which is offered daily in the Church is not something different from the sacrifice which Christ Himself offered, but it is its memory."[100] Before the great Protestant controversies had arisen, Saint Thomas, without peril of being misunderstood, could still make that extremely clear distinction between the sacrifice on the Cross and its memory on the altars of the Church. Mass, for him, is a *commemoratio*. This is the radical distinction between the sacrifice of the Cross and the sacrifice of the Eucharist; but we have to know what Saint Thomas meant by *commemoratio*. The question at issue then is not whether it be a *commemoratio*, but what kind of *commemoratio* it is.

16

The Sacrifice of the Cross

My readers may be surprised to have been kept waiting until now for the one great thing around which everything connected with the Eucharist centers—the sacrifice of the Cross, Christ's natural sacrifice. Would it not have been more helpful to have discussed this all-important matter in our very first chapter, since we have hardly been able so far to write a single page without referring to the sacrifice of the Cross? But this book, let me say it once more, is for the believer to whom the idea of the sacrifice of the Cross is familiar; its object is to help us to visualize the Eucharist in its true setting. The Cross is more truly the center than the beginning of the sacramental system; there is accordingly no lack of sound tactics if we pass through many a theological rampart before we come to the great citadel which dominates everything, the doctrine of Christ's sacrifice on Calvary. We have spoken of that mystery very often, now we come face to face with its native beauty, after having admired its reflections throughout the sacramental realm.

Our modern theologians are wont to debate at great length on the nature of sacrifice in the abstract, and to apply their *a priori* conclusions on the essence of sacrifice in general to the

Christian sacrifice, both natural and sacramental. It is remarkable, however, that among the vast theological labors of Saint Thomas such an investigation into the nature of sacrifice finds no place. He does not seem to have felt the need of it. What he says of sacrifice in the earlier parts of the *Summa* is part of his theology of the virtue of religion; as religion, again, is part of the moral virtue of justice. He remains extremely sober in his desire for investigating the nature of the sacrifice. I do not think I am alone in feeling that the theology of the Christian sacrifice has gained very little from the modern speculations on the nature of sacrifice in general. We surely know best what a sacrifice really is from the inspired literature of our Scriptures; the Christian sacrifice, with its special rites, stands apart on its own merits. It would certainly be dangerous to formulate a theory of the sacrifice quite independent of that immense sacrificial life which has gone on for thousands of years under God's sanction and direction, and to apply that formula to the divinely instituted sacrifices. It would be an attempt to explain the greater thing by the smaller, the divine institution by the human custom; certainly no theory of sacrifice could ever adequately meet the case of Christ's sacrifice on the Cross. It is a sacrifice so entirely *sui generis* that it has to be defined by itself.

The Scriptures assure us that sacrifice is a mode of divine worship which is absolute, in the sense that God alone may be honored in such a way. We know, again from our Scriptures, that in many sacrifices there is destruction of the living organism, though there are other sacrifices without such destruction. There is in all these sacrifices described in the Bible this all-important element, which we so often overlook, its covenanted acceptance by God. God is willing to receive a definite kind of homage; man will never be able to win God's favor through mere slaughterings of his precious herds, his sacrifice must be a pre-arranged transaction between God and man. This most important factor ought to be enough to make us wary in laying down *a priori* maxims on the nature of sacrifice. There is, moreover, this further circumstance, that the whole ancient sacrificial rite was figurative of Christ's sacrifice on the Cross. This means that we are to explain the ancient sacrifices through the sacrifice of the Cross and not *vice versa*. We are dealing with the supernatural, the divinely established, the divinely revealed, in this matter of sacrifice; and the speculations of natural theology ought to be subservient to the historic rites revealed by God Himself.

There is in the sacrifices of the Levitic legislation a definiteness of procedure which has all the character of a sacramental institution. We have heard Saint Thomas more than once speak of the ancient sacrifices as sacraments. They are circumscribed by conditions of time and place, as well as ceremonial; not any and every kind of man's generosity in God's service may claim the name of sacrifice. They are truly institutional religion, in the orthodox sense of that much-abused word, because as forms of worship they are independent of the subjective enthusiasm of religious feeling. They have a merit of their own, a power of pleasing God described in the oldest ritual phrases of the religious language of the world; they are essentially "a most sweet savor in the sight of the Lord, because it is His oblation."[101]

This expression, "savor of sweetness," runs through the whole sacrificial theology of the ancient Law. It is a phrase of such fixity, recurring so often, that in it we may surely discover the true meaning of sacrifice. The victim itself sends up to heaven a sweet perfume which is pleasing to the Lord God Almighty. "And Noah built an altar unto the Lord: and taking of all cattle and fowls that were clean, offered holocausts upon the altar. And the Lord smelled a sweet savor."[102] Some people might be tempted to accuse this sacrificial language in the Bible of gross materialism. There is certainly a definite material content in the divinely instituted sacrifices of the past; but that very "odor of sweetness" which ascends to God from the burnt offering is a revelation to us of God's ways and preferences.

If I may philosophize in my turn, let me say that a sacrifice is an act of religion, and therefore an act of justice, rendering to God what is His due. It is not directly an act of fortitude or of temperance or of prudence; but it is a simple act of fair and just dealing with God, wherein man, and even beast, is made to contribute to the recognition of God's sovereignty over all flesh. Even an heroic deed of fortitude in the service of God is not necessarily a sacrifice. Indeed, a sacrifice need not be a difficult thing, or a painful thing, but it must be a just thing and a true thing, rendering to God the things that are God's, in the manner in which He wills and decrees. To entirely spiritualize the oblation and make of it exclusively an act of the created mind and will would be the abolition of the sacrifice; all sacrifices are of the things that are bodily.

The hieratic phrase "odor of sweetness" is applied by Saint Paul to Christ on the Cross: "Christ also hath loved us and hath delivered Himself for us, an oblation and a sacrifice to God for an odor of sweetness."[103] We need hardly defend the old Christian tradition, as it has not really suffered diminution in spite of the great religious upheavals that have rent Christianity; I mean the belief that Christ's death on the Cross is a perfect and complete sacrifice, and that He is our High Priest through the offering of Himself as a victim to God on the Cross. To give to Christ's crucifixion and death only moral worth, even if it be to an infinite degree, is not the whole of Christianity; there is something besides the moral worth of the suffering and dying Christ, there is the sacrifice. Christ's death on the Cross was truly a ritual act, as it was done at the time, in the manner, in the circumstances, ordained by the Father, and foreshadowed by all the ancient sacrifices. To make of the crucified Christ anything less than a victim, in the ceremonial sense of the word, is to bring down His death to the human plane.

My purpose in this chapter is not so much to establish the sacrificial nature of the crucifixion—how can any Catholic doubt it after a tradition of two thousand years?—as to show the definiteness and the bodily nature of that sacrifice. There is a real danger besetting us in our own days, that of over-spiritualizing the Incarnation and its circumstances, of attaching value only to such things in Christ as may be called His spiritual acts.

The sacrifice of the Cross is not primarily definable in terms of spirit, but in terms of the body; it is not the heroic fortitude of Christ on the Cross which constitutes the sacrifice, but the material fact—we need not hesitate to use the word—of the pouring out of His Blood. There is in the sacrifice of the Cross, as well as in the ancient sacrifices, an element of absolute stability, the Body of the victim; and from that there rises to heaven the odor of sweetness. The more perfect sacrifice is the one which is of the holier and cleaner body; and if we have a Body of holiness and purity absolutely divine, we have the sacrifice of infinite worth.

Let us hear Saint Thomas describing those qualities of Christ's flesh which make it a most perfect sacrifice. An objector says that Christ's passion on the Cross ought not to be considered in the light of a sacrifice, because human flesh was never offered up in the ancient sacrifices, which were all of them figures of Christ. As on the Cross we have only Christ's flesh as a possible sacrifice, are we not compelled to drop entirely the idea of sacrifice out of the crucifixion? Such is the drift of the objector's argument, if not his very words. Now for the answer:

Although the reality ought to correspond with the figure in some respect, this need not be in every respect, because the reality ought to be greater than the type. It was, therefore, quite fitting that the figure of this sacrifice, through which the flesh of Christ is offered for us, was not the flesh of men, but of other animals that signified the flesh of Christ, which is the most perfect sacrifice. Firstly, indeed, because being the flesh belonging to a human nature, it is offered up with great congruity for men, and is partaken of by them in the sacrament. Secondly, being a passible and a mortal flesh it was apt for immolation. Thirdly, being a flesh without sin, it had efficacy for washing away sins. Fourthly, being the very flesh of the One who was offering it up, it was acceptable to God on account of the unspeakable charity of Him who thus offered it.

Whence Saint Augustine says in his Fourth Book on the Trinity: "Is there anything more fitly taken by men and offered up for them than human flesh? Is there anything more apt for this immolation than mortal flesh? Is there anything so clean, with such power of cleansing away the sins of men, as that flesh, born in a womb without the least stain of carnal lust, nay, born in the womb of a Virgin? And can anything be offered up and be accepted with such grace as the flesh of our sacrifice, which has become the body of our Priest?"[104]

Here Saint Augustine, the idealist, and Saint Thomas, the solid realist, are at one in their worship of that most perfect sacrifice, Christ's flesh.

Are we, then, in that furnace of charity, the passion and death of Christ, to separate the physical element from the spiritual element, assigning to the flesh the role of sacrifice?

Saint Thomas boldly makes this separation. In the Forty-Eighth Question of the Third Part of the *Summa* he analyzes the five ways in which Christ's Passion brings about our salvation, namely through merit, satisfaction, sacrifice, redemption and efficiency. The question arises, are these only five different aspects of one and the same thing; or more to our point, is sacrifice the same thing as merit, as satisfaction, as redemption? The answer keeps them all well apart.

> The Passion of Christ, with regard to His divinity, acts by way of efficiency; with regard to the will of Christ's soul, it acts by way of merit; considered as something within Christ's very flesh, it acts by way of satisfaction, inasmuch as through it we are liberated from the burden of punishment; insomuch as through it we are set free from the slavedom of guilt it acts by way of redemption; but it acts by way of sacrifice inasmuch as through it we are reconciled to God.[105]

Saint Thomas evidently makes Christ's flesh the bearer of that wonderful mission, His sacrificial mission. All things in the Passion were not directly sacrificial, because there were mighty things of the spirit, which, being of the spirit, could not properly be called sacrifice; not in His spirit, but in His flesh did Christ feel the burden that was put on Him by the Father.

Though we may separate the elements of sacrifice in Christ's Passion from its other elements, we do not, of course, isolate it. Everything that contributes to the sanctity and the holiness of the victim is undoubtedly an addition to the value of that sacrifice. But it is certain, by all theological principles, that not all of Christ's activity here on earth has in any way the character of sacrifice. His long life in poverty at Nazareth is decidedly not the sacrifice of the New Law; His Baptism and His fast, His patient endurance of persecution during the three years of

His public life, are not the sacrifice of the New Law. So much is admitted by the consensus of Catholic thought. The further distinction which Saint Thomas seems to make, and which I have quoted, analyzes Christ's Passion itself, and separates the sacrificial elements from the non-sacrificial elements even in that supreme moment of Christ's career. But all that previous sanctity, all the charity of the Cross, were focused on that one element, sacrifice, because they made the victim holy beyond words. If they were not the sacrifice they were the sanctity of the victim, they were the glory of that life which was to be laid down in the sacrifice; and the nobler the life, the more precious the laying down of it, the greater the sacrifice.

Another passage of Saint Thomas which clearly distinguishes even in the Passion of Christ between sacrifice and other saving powers in that great combat of the Son of God with evil is found in the Fourth Article of the Forty-Ninth Question:

> Whether through the Passion of Christ we have been reconciled to God?
>
> My answer is that the Passion of Christ is the cause of our reconciliation with God in a twofold manner. In one way because it takes away sin through which men are made enemies of God.... In another way through its being a sacrifice most acceptable unto God, for this is properly the effect of a sacrifice that through it God be appeased.

A simple consideration will make it clear how in that infinitely great thing, the Passion of Christ, sacrifice must be distinguished from other things. Mankind as a race has been redeemed once for all by Christ's death on the Cross; the power of Satan as a monarchy of evil has been broken. Now this redemption cannot be repeated, even sacramentally, because it is not applicable to individual souls, it is concerned with the whole of mankind. It lies, so to speak, at the basis of all other dealings of God with men. Very often the terms "redemption," "satisfaction," and "sacrifice" are interchanged, as, indeed, they are so closely united in that one central thing, the Passion of Christ; and it is commonly said that we are redeemed through Christ's sacrifice on the Cross. But precision becomes necessary when we are bent on seeing everything in its proper setting; and sacrifice, even of the Cross, is not quite the same thing as redemption by the Cross. "To be saved" may be considered as the most universal result of the Cross. Let us remember that, in the doctrine of Saint Thomas, salvation is through five different ways.

Christ merited for Himself that supreme exaltation of which Saint Paul speaks in the Epistle to the Philippians: "He humbled Himself, becoming obedient unto death, even to the death of the Cross. For which cause, God also hath exalted Him, and hath given Him a name which is above all names."[106] Here, again, we have an element in Christ's Passion which cannot be strictly described under the heading "sacrifice," as Saint Thomas points out so clearly in Article Four of the Twenty-Second Question of Part Three. Here an objector says that Christ's priesthood, exercised in His sacrifice on the Cross, was beneficial to Himself; because through the Cross Christ merited exaltation for Himself and not only for others. This inference Saint Thomas denies, quoting the Council of Ephesus, which excommunicates anyone who says that Christ offered up sacrifices for Himself. Christ's priesthood and sacrifice are all for the benefit of man. This gives Saint Thomas an opportunity for distinguishing glory from glory in Christ's death on the Cross:

> In the offering of a sacrifice by any priest we may consider two things—namely, the sacrifice itself, which is offered, and the devotion of the one who offers. Now the proper effect of

the priesthood is the one that comes from the sacrifice itself. But Christ merited through His passion the glory of His Resurrection, not in virtue of the sacrifice, which is offered up by way of atonement, but through that devotion of His with which, out of charity, He bore humbly His passion.[107]

We may, then, without going further into this matter, take it for granted that even in the Passion there were definite elements that constituted the sacrifice, and these specific things are directly represented in the Eucharistic sacrifice.

The very nature of sacrifice implies a gift to God, and this aspect of donation is constantly mentioned by Saint Thomas when he distinguishes sacrifice from the other splendors of Christ's passion.

This is properly the effect of a sacrifice, that through it God be appeased; just as a man is ready to forgive an injury done him on account of some acceptable service rendered him. Thus it is said in the First Book of Kings, chapter 26: *If the Lord stir thee up against me, let Him accept of sacrifice.* And so in the same way what Christ suffered was so great a good that, on account of that good found in human nature, God has been appeased for all the offenses of mankind, with regard at least to those who are linked up with the Christ who suffered.[108]

The feature in the passion which seems especially the gift of Christ to His Father, and which therefore more particularly contains the element of sacrifice, is the laying down of His life: "Therefore doth the Father love Me: because I lay down my life that I may take it again. No man taketh it away from Me: but I lay it down of Myself. And I have power to lay it down: and I have power to take it up again. This commandment have I received of my Father."[109] But this laying down of His life is the same as the pouring out of His life-blood. So we see Saint

Paul, in the Epistle to the Hebrews, making the sacrifice of the Cross consist in the Blood. The texts are well known; they are truly a hymn of Christ's great sacrifice on the Cross.

> But Christ, being come an high priest of the good things to come, by a greater and more perfect tabernacle, not made with hand, that is, not of this creation: neither by the blood of goats or of calves, but by His own blood, entered once into the Holies, having obtained eternal redemption. For if the blood of goats and of oxen and the ashes of an heifer, being sprinkled, sanctify such as are defiled, to the cleansing of the flesh: how much more shall the blood of Christ, who by the Holy Spirit offered Himself unspotted to God, cleanse our conscience from dead works, to serve the living God? And therefore He is the mediator of the new testament: that by means of His death for the redemption of those transgressions which were under the former testament, they that are called may receive the promise of eternal inheritance.[110]
>
> Nor yet that He should offer Himself often, as the high priest entereth into the Holies every year with the blood of others. For then He ought to have suffered often from the beginning of the world. But now once, at the end of ages, He hath appeared for the destruction of sin by the sacrifice of Himself. And, as it is appointed unto men once to die, and after this the judgement; so also Christ was offered once to exhaust the sins of many. The second time He shall appear without sin to them that expect Him unto salvation.[111]

Much could be said on these inspired words; but if they make clear one thing it is this, the sacrificial nature of the Passion of Christ, and, above all, the sacrificial nature of the pouring out of His Blood. This latter feature in Christ's Passion stands out as the supreme sacerdotal act; and there is no doubt it is there we must find the essence of the great Christian sacrifice. This is what is represented in the Eucharist; this is what was foreshadowed in all the sacrifices of the Old Law.

We have come to elements which are clearly traceable, as you may trace the course of a river which springs from the mountains, flows through a lake, and comes out of the lake to continue its long course towards the ocean, gladdening on its way the cities of men. The first portion of the stream we may identify with the figurative sacrifice of the Old Law; the lake, with the stream clearly moving through it, even with a diversity in the color of the water, is the sacrificial element in Christ's glorious Passion; the third, and the longest stretch of the river, is the Eucharistic sacrifice.

17

Transubstantiation

Nothing could give us a clearer insight into the Eucharistic doctrine than the position which Transubstantiation holds. We have already quoted Saint Thomas telling us that the power which changes comes after the power of signification;[112] in other words, the whole external sacramental action in words and deeds signifies one thing, and one thing only, the Body of Christ and the Blood of Christ. This is the oldest form under which we meet the Eucharist in Christian tradition. The Church has simply given a literal interpretation to the words of the Eucharistic rite. It was not said first that bread was being changed into Christ's Body and that wine was being changed into Christ's Blood; what was said first and is always said first, is: "This is my Body, this is my Blood"; the additional concept of change may almost be called an afterthought. Yet the Church could not give the reason of her great sacramental utterances without giving as her explanation this mysterious change, which is so near to the heart of the main mystery itself that it may truly be called a part of it. The substance of bread is changed into Christ's Body and the substance of wine is changed into Christ's Blood. Transubstantiation, then, is not so much the sacrament, as the divinely revealed explanation of the truth of the sacrament. Transubstantiation is not the Eucharistic sacrifice, but it is the hidden power that makes the sacrifice a reality and not a mere symbol.

An instance from another portion of Catholic theology makes this relative position of Transubstantiation in the Eucharistic mystery quite comprehensible. Theologians hold that God directly creates every human soul and unites it with the human embryo. Now this doctrine of God's direct creative act in producing the soul is not one that stands in the first rank of truths; but it is a postulate which has to be brought in as the only satisfactory hypothesis in the explanation of man's nature. A doctrine that stands in the first rank of evidence is this, that man, as we know him, is endowed with an intellectual soul; this is the thing that matters to us, and which is directly evident to us. Yet when we come to ask the question, "How does this intellectual principle come to be in man?" the only answer is this: God creates it in every instance.

So it is with Transubstantiation. The doctrine that stands in the first rank of evidence is the Body and Blood of Christ given to us in the form of sacrifice. This is the mystery we approach directly; we enter into it at once; nothing prepares us for it except the authority of Christ and His Church. In matters of the Eucharist we immediately find ourselves at the center of the mystery; we stumble, so to speak, without any warning on the sacrament of Christ's Body and Christ's Blood. The holiest thing is the first thing we meet. We do not bring Christ down from heaven, we do not raise Him up from the depths, through the sacramental signification; He is in our hands and in our mouths before we know where we are. The sacrifice is consummated through the lightning power of the sacramental words that announce it. Overawed, as it were, by the might of the thing that has happened, we ask: "How did it happen?"

The answer is—Transubstantiation. As in the case of the human personality giving such evidence of an intellectual soul, the unseen fiat of God in a mother's womb is the only satisfactory way of accounting for that splendor which meets me in a creature so perfect in mind and body; so is Transubstantiation at the root of all Eucharistic blessings. Transubstantiation is not, and could not be, the same thing as the Eucharist, whether in its aspect of sacrifice or of food; but it is at the root of the sacrament, deep down in the abyss of being, where God's omnipotence is supreme.

There have been theologians, more devout than learned, who have given this picture of the Eucharistic sacrifice. In every sacrifice, they said, the first thing is the bringing in of the victim; then there is the consecration of the victim; and thirdly there is its immolation. They thought that Transubstantiation corresponded exactly with the first stage of a sacrifice, the bringing in of a victim, as through it Christ's Body and Blood were brought on to our altars. But who does not see how infelicitous a role Transubstantiation is thus given? It places it in the first rank of sacramental truth, instead of making it the explanation of sacramental truth. In such an hypothesis Transubstantiation would be the sacrament itself; we would have for sacrament, not a divine thing, but the act of God itself. It is as if we made that act by which He creates every individual soul part and parcel of the human nature of the people we meet. This, of course, would be an unpardonable confusion of thought. Let us say it once more, Transubstantiation is not the same thing as the sacrament of Christ's Body and Christ's Blood; those things we hold in virtue of sacramental formulas of consecration; but it is the hidden act of God, which is absolutely indispensable if the sacramental consecration be true.

Saint Thomas sums this up in one beautiful sentence in the

Seventy-Fifth Question, Article Two, which sets out to prove that the substance of bread and wine does not remain after the consecration. "God has yoked His divinity, that is to say, His divine power, to bread and wine, not so that they should remain in the sacrament, but so as to make from them His body and blood."[113] The power we call Transubstantiation is a transient act, while the sacrament abides for a time, more or less prolonged. This power does not remain in the sacrament, but the Body and Blood of Christ remain. This consideration should be enough to make it clear to us what a difference there is between Transubstantiation and the sacrament properly so called; and to show what confusion would arise in our Eucharistic theology if we made Transubstantiation stand for an element in the essence of the sacrifice.

After these considerations on the comparatively relative position of Transubstantiation in the Eucharistic doctrine, let us come now to a few aspects which will endear to us this divine thing, Transubstantiation, as being the most simple— nay, even the most beautiful explanation of all we know of the Eucharistic mystery. If it is not the sacrament itself, it is certainly the sweet and gracious mother of the sacrament. In its simplicity it has all the grace and charm of eternal wisdom.

I think the best way to make clear to the reader the glory of Transubstantiation is to point out that after Christ, the Son of God, had performed the great deed of the first consecration at the Last Supper the miracle was complete, and nothing new has happened since. The circumstance that thousands of priests consecrate today in all parts of the world is no new marvel. Transubstantiation contained the whole marvel from the beginning. Transubstantiation is the power of Christ to change bread into His Body and wine into His Blood. Now this is an absolute power, not limited in any way. If the thing can be done once, it can be done always, in every place, wherever bread and wine are found. There can be no new difficulties, because the power of Transubstantiation is concerned directly with the whole species of bread and wine. If you once admit that Christ has power to raise up the dead, if He had in fact raised up a dead man but once, you are not surprised if He raises up a hundred or a thousand or a million dead men; it is all the same to Him, if He has power over death. It would, indeed, be a childish attitude of mind to think that it is more difficult for God to heal ten lepers than to heal one, to raise up ten dead men than to raise up one.

So with this power of Transubstantiation: if one piece of bread and one cup of wine may be changed by Christ into His Body and Blood, why not a hundred pieces, a hundred cups? The mystery is always the same. There is no more reason to be astonished at the number of Eucharistic sacrifices offered up than at the number of Baptisms administered in the world. If there is the power in the Church to regenerate into spiritual life one soul—and this power is tremendous, much greater than we think—every soul may be brought under the influence of Baptismal regeneration. If Christ, holding the bread and cup of wine, could declare them to be the same thing as the Body and the Blood that were at that moment constituent elements of His living Personality, the same declaration may be repeated with the same truthfulness, because the underlying power remains unaltered, undiminished: this is Transubstantiation.

The wisdom of the Church in declaring Transubstantiation to be the only explanation she has of her mystery of faith may be better appreciated if we compare it with another hypothesis, excogitated by certain thinkers, perhaps more ardent than illumined, who wanted to find a satisfactory answer to the question of how Christ is present on so many altars. They have recourse to metaphysical theories on the nature of space and place; they say, in so many words, that the Body of Christ could come into every corner of the world simultaneously, as possessing a kind of multiplicity of presence. Such a theory, if it mean anything at all, would certainly imply that Christ, in His bodily nature, would be moving backward and forward in space with incredible rapidity so as to be present on every altar at the moment of consecration.

This is a bewildering way of explaining the Real Presence, and the fact of its having been sponsored by pious men does not make it less confusing. It would make of the Eucharist a thing of material mobility and velocity. Not so Transubstantiation.

Wherever a priest, in the name of Christ, pronounces the sacramental consecration, the substance of the bread and the substance of the wine are changed into the substance of Christ's Body and the substance of Christ's Blood. There is no bringing down from heaven of the Body and Blood of Christ; this is not the Eucharist; but Christ's Body and Christ's Blood are truly produced in an act of divine power, as grace is produced in the human soul at Baptism. The wonderful thing produced in the Eucharist is, of course, far greater than that produced in Baptism; but in both cases there is a production—nay, in both cases there is a change. In Baptism the soul is changed from sin unto grace; in the Eucharist the substance of bread and the substance of wine are changed into the substance of Christ's Body and the substance of Christ's Blood. This is not only a change into a greater thing than Baptismal grace, it is also a greater change, because the whole reality is changed, down to the very roots of being. But, let us repeat it, in both cases, in Baptism and in the Eucharist, the sacrament is the changing of something.

Multiplicity of the sacramental act, whether in time or

space, adds nothing to the sacrament. We do not say, or ought not to say, that Christ is on many altars, as in so many places, but as in the sacrament. Here are Saint Thomas's own words:

> The Body of Christ is not in this sacrament in the manner in which a body is in a place, having its dimensions commensurate with that place; but it is present in a certain special manner, which belongs exclusively to this sacrament. So we say that the Body of Christ is on many altars, not as in so many places, but as in the sacrament; by which we do not mean that Christ is there only in a sign, although the sacrament be of the genus sign; but we understand that His Body is there according to the manner proper to the sacrament.[114]

The uninitiated may be startled when they read this frank statement, yet such is the emphatic and unswerving teaching of the great Doctor. For him it is simply unthinkable—nay, it implies a metaphysical contradiction—that the Body of Christ should ever be considered as moving simultaneously from place to place, or as overcoming, in some miraculous manner, all spatial hindrances. Transubstantiation is infinitely simpler. Wherever bread and wine are found, their hidden substance is transubstantiated into the hidden substance of Christ's Body and Blood, in the same way as was done at the Last Supper. This is what Saint Thomas means when he says that the Body of Christ is not in a place but in a sacrament. The Body of Christ is not taken hold of, hurried through space and put into a definite place on a definite altar, this is not Eucharist at all; but the divine invocation, as the words of consecration are so often called by the Fathers, makes the substance of a definite bread and the substance of a definite cup of wine into something new. And what is that new thing? It is simply that thing which is in heaven, the Body and Blood of Christ, but which has not left heaven for one instant.

The usual term which emphasizes the difference between the Catholic and the Protestant view of the Eucharist is "Real Presence." Christ's Body and Blood are really present; nay, the whole Christ is really present, as will be seen in a later chapter. But, while holding to our belief in this Real Presence, we say with great attention to accuracy of thought that Christ is not on the altar as in a place. No doubt for most men to be present somewhere is the same thing as being placed there. There is, however, a vast difference. The bread and wine before the consecration are truly on the altar as in a place, they are put on the altar by the minister. What are called the accidents of bread and wine, the external appearances, remain on the altar during the sacrifice, even after the consecration. But there is something, an inward element of reality in that bread and wine which the sacramental consecration changes into a much greater reality, Christ's Body and Blood; and that change is the only reason why Christ is there. Christ is on the altar as in a sacrament, according to the precise expression of Saint Thomas, in virtue of this hidden change within the nature of the bread and wine. Here, we have the most sublime verification of the axiom, that the sacrament produces the thing which it signifies; here it signifies the Body and Blood of Christ, and it produces It.

As already insinuated, the difference between the Eucharist and the other sacraments is not one of kind, but one of degree. They are all of them powers of changing. In the other sacraments the change is in the soul of men, in this sacrament the change is in the very elements, bread and wine. Perhaps we think it a less incredible marvel, a lighter tax on our faith, that the soul of the infant, through Baptismal regeneration, should receive the life of God, the imprint of Christ, the likeness of the angels, than that bread and wine should be made into the

Holy Thing that was on the Cross, that was poured out on Calvary. But Saint Thomas speaks of the two marvels in the same breath, as if they were not essentially different, as if the one ought to prepare us for the other: "What the power of the Holy Spirit is with regard to the water of Baptism, this the true body of Christ is with regard to the appearances of bread and wine."[115] Once we admit that God dwells in material things as a source of eternal life—and this is the very concept of the Christian sacrament—have we not admitted the Eucharistic mystery, the Real Presence? The Thing which is Christ's Body and Christ's Blood is under the material appearances of bread and wine.

The Christian sacraments are infinitely fertile things. The external sign, in the formal word and material element, becomes fruitful beyond calculation in the realm of grace. Is it not a trite metaphor with the ancient Fathers to call the baptismal waters a mother's womb? The Eucharist is the most fertile of sacraments, yet its fertility belongs to the same secret source of life. The classical Catholic tradition conceives the Eucharist almost exclusively from this point of view, the wonderful productiveness of Christ's power. Christ's Eucharistic Body is produced in the manner in which His divine hands produced bread when He multiplied the loaves. The older thinkers are not hampered by what might be called the spatial difficulty in the Eucharist; they saw no such difficulty, because there is none. The power of Christ to change bread and wine is the only thing they knew of, and their Eucharistic theology was accordingly simple in the extreme: they believed in the power of the sacrament to produce what it signifies.

There is in the metaphysical presentment of the Eucharist by Saint Thomas a wonderful calmness of outlook, and a complete avoidance of the worrying complexity of thought from which even good theologians have not always been able to escape. This is aptly illustrated in two of his answers to objections.

> Through the power of a finite agent no one form can be changed into another form, no one matter can be changed into another matter; but such a change can be effected through the power of an infinite agent, whose action extends over the whole realm of being, because the nature of being is common to both forms and both matters. What is being in one, the author of being can change into that which is being in another, by removing that which made the difference.[116]

When Saint Thomas says that God has power over the whole realm of being he has truly given us the last word in this matter; and yet how simple this last word is: *Habet actionem in totum ens* (His action extends over the whole realm of being).

Another such serene utterance is concerned with the cessation of the sacramental presence. When the appearances of bread and wine lose their identity, as they must do sooner or later, the Body and Blood also cease to be present. How do Body and Blood cease to be there? How do they depart?

> The Body of Christ remains in the sacrament, not only for the day after the consecration, but even until a future time, as long as the sacramental appearances remain. If they cease, then the Body of Christ ceases to be under them, not because the Body of Christ depends on them, but because the relationship of Christ's Body to those appearances is taken away. In this way God simply ceases to be the Lord of a creature which ceases to exist.[117]

May it not be said that the Eucharistic mystery is really no exception to those laws of being, both finite and infinite, created and increate, which Catholic theology has studied and enunciated with such success? But if, instead of metaphysics, we were to use sentiment and imagination in giving the account of our faith in this mystery, should we not very soon find ourselves hopelessly entangled?

18

"Difficulties"

$\mathbf{W}$e are almost forced to smile when we see the apparently casual way in which Saint Thomas treats the most burning of all spiritual questions: "Whether the Body of Christ be in this sacrament in very truth?"[118] It is by no means the first thing he asks; this great question comes about midway in his treatment of the Eucharist. Till then he has been busy showing that the Eucharist is truly a sacrament; and it looks as if this important Article were merely one link in a chain of reasoning through which the true sacramental character of the Eucharist is established. For that purpose he has to prove the all-important fact that Christ's Body and Blood are in the sacrament, literally and in very truth. Yet there is profound wisdom in such an arrangement, and no one who has given much time to that part of the *Summa* will ever say that the theology of Saint Thomas on the Eucharist is not complete and perfectly balanced. It is a monument of spiritual and mystical insight. But the monument is not a pyramid, standing in isolated greatness in the midst of the desert; it is rather the citadel which crowns the city, I mean the whole sacramental theology which surrounds it, leading up to it and away from it.

After giving the reasons why the Body of Christ is in truth

in the sacrament, he concludes:

> Some men, not bearing in mind these things, have contended
> that the Body and Blood of Christ are in this sacrament only
> as in a sign; but this is to be rejected as heretical, it being
> contrary to the words of Christ. And therefore Berengarius,
> who was the first author of such a heresy, has been obliged to
> recant his error and to make profession of the truth of the
> faith.[119]

When we remember what theological storms have raged
around this very sacrament since that time, the serenity of
Saint Thomas produces mild astonishment. Human imagination
was roused one day like a giant who had been slumbering after
excess of wine. It broke all it could, and filled the world with
the ruins of the Catholic altars.

Yet not one of those difficulties which, a few centuries after
Saint Thomas, sent half of Western Christendom into a frenzy
of denials and even blasphemies, was unknown in the days of
the great thinker, or was undiscussed in all the contemporary
schools of theology. Indeed, the medieval way of stating such
difficulties was astonishingly frank and thorough. But at no
time did the philosophers of the ages of faith come across one
single thing that could be truly called an impossibility, or, as
they would have named it, a *contradictio in terminis*, a contradiction in terms, an incompatibility of concepts.

There is great wisdom in their selection of the arena for
the battle. For them the problems, if problems there were, had
reference essentially—nay, exclusively—to the constitution of
the material body. Admitting the power of creation, it was no
real difficulty for them to believe that God should change any
one thing into another thing: that He should change water
into wine, or bread and wine into any other substance; all this

is implied in the concept of creative power.

In the case of Eucharistic Transubstantiation the departure from their normal thinking lay in this, that in the very change there is a selection of extraordinary penetration: in the same bodily thing one thing is changed and the other thing remains unchanged; furthermore, the change results in a new thing, not in its complete material circumstances, but with a wonderful detachment from any material circumstances. Not the whole bread and the whole wine are changed, but the substance only of the bread and the substance only of the wine; what are called the accidents, the external appearances, remain and become solid realities in their own right. Again, the Body of Christ and the Blood of Christ, which are the new thing after the Transubstantiation, are not there in the natural mode in which bodily things occupy room in spatial surroundings.

This division of reality from reality is the only difficulty for the thinker; the change itself is admitted by implication the moment creation is admitted. All the speculation of the Schoolmen in Eucharistic matters is concerned with change, not with space, as is too often the case in more recent treatment of the subject. Now Saint Thomas frankly admits that in this change there are certain issues not contained in the ordinary principles of the doctrine of creation:

> In this change there are several things which are more difficult than in creation, in which this alone is the difficulty, that something is made out of nothing; but, after all, this is the manner of production proper to the First Cause, which presupposes nothing else. But in this change the difficulty lies not only in the circumstance that one being in its totality be changed into another being in its totality, so that nothing of the former being remains (which mode of production, indeed, is not usual with any cause); but there is the additional diffi-

culty, namely, that the accidents remain when the substance has been changed; and there are many other difficult matters of which we shall have to treat later on. We use, however, the word "change," with regard to the sacrament, and not with regard to creation.[120]

We know, of course, what Saint Thomas means when he calls a thing "difficult." The difficulty is not on the part of God, but on the part of the human intellect. Besides that, nothing disposes bodily matter like bread and wine for a change at the same time so absolute and yet so selective. For the power of the Creator, no doubt, this is child's-play, as is everything else in the material world. "This change takes place, not through any passive potentiality of the creature, but through the sole active power of the Creator."[121]

The Catholic theologian, then, has to admit the difficulty; but let him keep it in its proper place. Once more, I would remind the reader that everything in the Eucharist, as in other sacraments, centers round the idea of change, either spiritual or material. Can our souls be changed through the baptismal waters and the Holy Spirit? Can our wills be changed through the absolving power of penance? Can the innermost portion of our spirit be changed? Can it be sealed by the Holy Spirit in the sacrament of Confirmation? These are mighty questions indeed. The Catholic Church answers them all in the affirmative.

The Eucharistic change is concerned directly with the elements themselves. Can bread and wine be changed into a divine Thing? Again the Church says: Yes. The difference between the Eucharist and the other sacraments is not a radical difference, but only an accidental difference.

This sacrament differs from the other sacraments in two ways: Firstly, because this sacrament is completed in the consecration of the matter, while the other sacraments are perfected in the use of the matter. Secondly, because in the other sacraments the consecration of the matter is merely a certain blessing, from which the matter derives instrumentally a spiritual power ... but in this sacrament the consecration of the matter consists in a miraculous change of the substance which can be accomplished by God alone.[122]

The receiving of the Eucharist by the faithful is, of course, an additional sacramental circumstance. Protestantism has located the Eucharistic change in the soul only, when Christ is received by faith; Catholicism, with a deeper insight into spiritual realities, places the Eucharistic change, before all things and above all things, in the Eucharistic elements.

After all, are the changes of the individual soul such an easy matter? Why do we believe more readily in the conversion of a sinner than in the Eucharistic change, which is constantly called by Saint Thomas a *conversio*? Did we know the real workings of things, perhaps we might find it just as difficult to believe in spiritual conversion as in Transubstantiation, unless we had God's authority. Is there not a famous passage in the Gospels where Our Lord Himself appeals to God's omnipotence in order to explain moral conversion?

And Jesus seeing him (the young man) become sorrowful, said: How hardly shall they that have riches enter into the kingdom of God! For it is easier for a camel to pass through the eye of a needle than for a rich man to enter into the kingdom of God. And they that heard Him said: Who, then, can be saved? He said to them: The things that are impossible with men are possible with God.[123]

In this matter of the Eucharist, as in all matters of theology, we should be satisfied with such aspects of the doctrine as the most prudent Catholic mind accepts in all dutifulness of faith. This is particularly the case with the all-important question of the identity between Christ's natural Body and Christ's Eucharistic Body. This identity is no longer a difficulty of the material order, but it is really a point belonging directly to the metaphysics of being.

In what sense must we say that the Eucharistic Body is identical with the natural Body of Christ? That they are identical is the very point of this sacrament; yet even in this identity there is a possibility of difference.

Let us bear in mind that the Eucharistic Body of Christ is truly the result of a production, of a change. It is made; *conficitur* is the word used both in theology and the Liturgy. Saint Thomas is quite definite in giving to the Eucharistic Body one *esse* and to Christ's natural Body another *esse*. "Christ has not the same *esse* in Himself and under this sacrament, because when we say that He has an *esse* under the sacrament there is signified a relationship of Himself to the sacrament."[124]

It is difficult to render into English the full meaning of *esse*. "Mode of being" is perhaps the nearest approach to a satisfactory rendering. With perfect identity in everything, there is still this possible difference, there is another mode of being. In the Eucharist we have the Body of Christ and the Blood of Christ, but with a mode of being entirely different from that mode of being in which Christ was at the Last Supper, in which He is now in heaven.

I will now quote from the theologians of Salamanca, who indisputably form one of the most orthodox schools of Catholic thought. In their great work on the Eucharist they say, with charming liberality of theological manners:

> The opinion which one ought to prefer quite simply in this matter is the one which makes the thing more clear to the intellect, answering the difficulties which are brought forward.

This is particularly the task assigned to a theologian in matters of such difficulty. This we shall achieve, then, if we say that the term towards which the act of Transubstantiation tends is the Body and Blood of Christ, with a new substantial mode of being, a mode of being different from the one Christ has in heaven, a mode of being acquired (in the sacrament) through the change and in virtue of the change.... It is clear, then, that Christ, as He is in Himself and as He is in heaven in His natural mode of being, is really distinct from Himself in as far as He claims for Himself and owns that substantial mode of being which He has in the sacrament.[125]

The Spanish theologians evidently think that they are making a concession by allowing us to hold this difference in modes of being, one for the natural Christ, the other for the Eucharistic Christ. Yet they are persuaded that such a difference is essential to the true understanding of the Eucharistic change.

This duality in the mode of being—the natural mode and the sacramental mode—belongs to the heart of the mystery. We are really coming back here to the guiding thought of this whole book, the sacramental state.

For more than one believer, without being conscious of it, the Eucharistic Presence is nothing else than a natural presence under a thin disguise. Such, of course, is not the Catholic dogma. Sacraments, as has been said before, belong to a sphere of reality which has nothing in common with the natural plane of reality. Could Christ be present in His natural reality both in heaven and on earth? I speak now of His human presence. Saint Thomas would say that it is not possible. But why make the supposition? We are not treating of natural presences, but of sacramental presences, and the new substantial mode of being, spoken of by the theologians of Salamanca, is nothing else than the sacramental state, as opposed to the natural state of being. Here, again, perfect identity becomes possible through the very dissimilarity of the two states. All our troubles come from an indiscriminate use of ideas, in constantly making concepts which belong to the natural state of being do service for concepts which belong to the sacramental mode of being.

Another great commentator on Saint Thomas, Cardinal Cajetan, gives the theologian of the Eucharist this advice: not to proceed on absolute lines of thought, as he would do in the natural order of reality; but "with a light touch to discourse on the lines of the power of the sacraments and their order."[126]

In connection with the foregoing, we may add a consideration which will stand us in good stead when we come to the practical and daily use of the Holy Eucharist. Saint Thomas admits as a general principle that Christ's humanity, considered in its natural order, is something more important than the sacraments of His humanity: "*Ipsa humanitas potior est quam sacramenta humanitatis.*"[127] This, of course, applies directly to the Eucharist, for it is in connection with the Eucharist that Saint Thomas enunciates the axiom. It is difficult to render the adjective *potior*; it means something holding a higher place, being of greater importance, though it need not be superior in nature.

The occasion for Saint Thomas to say this is the necessity in which he finds himself to assign the rank, in the gradation of sin, for bad communions. To sin against Christ's divinity is the greatest sin; next comes the sin against Christ's humanity in His natural state; then the sin committed against the sacrament of Christ's humanity; and, finally, the sin against the ordinary creature. Sin committed against the sacrament of Christ's humanity, were it even a bad communion, is not so great as the sin committed by those who crucified Christ in His own nature. "The sin of those who killed Christ was much greater. Firstly, because that sin was against Christ's Body in its proper nature, but this sin is against Christ's Body under the sacramental species. Secondly, because that sin came from an intention of hurting Christ, but not this sin."[128]

Catholic theology would certainly lose much if at any time the relative position of the natural Christ and the Eucharistic Christ were habitually ignored.

19

Concomitance

More than once in the course of this book I have promised the reader a special chapter on the doctrine of Eucharistic concomitance. I have been conscious all along that, in order to make clear the sacramental character of the Eucharistic sacrifice, I have been silent about splendors of which every Catholic is instinctively aware. Those precious things, the Body and Blood of Christ in the Eucharist, are not isolated.

Now the doctrine of concomitance fully satisfies those anticipations and instincts of the Catholic mind. The word "concomitance" is often used by Saint Thomas. It has been given dogmatic value of the first rank by the Council of Trent. Though it has a very technical sound, it is in reality a most gracious word. Its Latin etymology signifies the act of walking along with someone as a companion: *concomitari*—the roots of which are *cum* (with) and *comes* (companion). Its theological meaning is this, that the Eucharistic Body and Blood of Christ are accompanied; they are not alone, they come, as it were, escorted by friends. Those holy things, Body and Blood, are like the center of a group; they are surrounded by other holy things, without which they do not exist.

But let us be less figurative in speech. Sacramental signification has a precise meaning and a definite result. In all the sacraments, except one, the sacramental signification and the sacramental result cover each other perfectly, so that there is nothing else except the directly sacramental thing. The exception is the Eucharist. The Eucharist is certainly the sacrament of the Body and Blood of Christ, of nothing more and nothing less. But as the Body and the Blood of Christ are not found isolated now, and in fact were not isolated at the Last Supper—the only time of their isolation being on Calvary, after Christ's death—the sacrament of the Eucharist has a concomitance, a cortege of splendors. The Body and Blood of Christ on the Christian altar are perfectly identical with the Body and Blood of Christ in heaven; therefore on the altar they are surrounded by all that surrounds them in the Person of Christ in heaven. But let us be very clear about this: this cortege of new splendors has nothing to do with the sacrament as such. Strictly speaking, the sacrament prescinds from them. The sacrament is only that which it signifies, and the signification is only of the Body and the Blood.

Three expressions meet the student of this part of theology at every turn, in the *Summa* and, as a matter of fact, in all theological works: *vi sacramenti, vi verborum, vi conversionis*; which mean, respectively, in virtue of the sacrament, in virtue of the words of consecration, and in virtue of change or Transubstantiation. Whatever is in the Eucharist as the result of one of these three is sacrament. Whatever else may happen to be in the consecrated bread and wine is there *vi concomitantiae*.

For a thing to be in the Eucharist in virtue of the sacrament is a profound concept; in fact the all-dominating idea in this divine matter is the importance of the relationship of signification. God Himself, according to Saint Thomas in a passage already quoted, acts sacramentally, not naturally, when He operates in the Eucharist. By *vi sacramenti* then is meant that special order of realities which we have so often described.

In virtue of the words we have in the Eucharist all those things, and only those things, which are contained in the formulas of consecration. Let us take those sacred phrases; let us give literal meaning to their every word, and we have the exact statement of what there is on the altar. To add a single word would be a blasphemous interference. The sacrament is everything which is expressed by those holy and terse utterances, the words of consecration.

In virtue of change we have this, that bread is transubstantiated into Christ's Body and that wine is transubstantiated into Christ's Blood, nothing more. By *vi conversionis* less is represented than by *vi verborum*, because the words of consecration may mean something more than body and blood. The change is the most limited thing in the Eucharistic process; it affects nothing except the material thing, and that in a very definite way. I say this because it is a debated point whether Christ's Hypostatic Union is in the Eucharist *vi verborum* or *vi concomitantiae*. It can certainly not be there *vi conversionis*; but it might be there *vi verborum*, for the consecration words might be so construed as not to be intelligible of a Body or a Blood not hypostatically united to the Godhead. Some theologians think that the possessive adjectives, *meum* and *mei*, in the consecration words, imply Hypostatic Union, as no Body or no Blood belonging to Christ is disunited from His divine Person. The Council of Trent seems to favor this opinion, as we shall see presently. My object here is to show that there ought to be a difference in the meanings attached to *vi verborum* and *vi conversionis*.

It is evident that the two expressions *vi verborum* and *vi conversionis* are contained under the more comprehensive expression *vi sacramenti*, which is directly opposed to that other term, *vi concomitantiae*. I ought to say that Saint Thomas generally adds an adjective, and speaks of *vi realis concomitantiae*, in virtue of a real concomitance, no doubt with a view to excluding a merely figurative or a merely moral association of realities.

In order to make it clear what is in the Eucharist *vi sacramenti*, Catholic theologians have reduced the Eucharistic realities to a kind of minimum, convinced as they are that in these sublime matters man has no right to go one single step beyond the meaning attached by God. They all exclude Christ's human Soul from the strictly sacramental content of the Eucharist. Not only are bread and wine not changed into Christ's Soul, but the Eucharist is something so immediately connected with Body and Blood that the very emphasis of this bodily aspect excludes the Soul. Bread and wine are changed into Christ's Body and Blood in a very precise manner, with just enough degree of being to make the words true, and nothing more.

"The form of bread," says Saint Thomas, "is changed into the form of Christ's Body, according as it gives corporeal being, but not according as it gives being animated by such a soul."[129] By "form" here is meant the substantial form, and anyone who knows anything about the scholastic theory of matter and form will readily see how Saint Thomas in this passage reduces the effect of Transubstantiation to the lowest minimum compatible with the meaning of the words of consecration. It is not my intention to enter into all the philosophic considerations raised by this attitude of Catholic theologians; enough for me to commend the extremely sound tradition in the Catholic school of the older type, not to speak where God Himself has not spoken. Moreover, it is through that distinction between the virtue of the sacrament and concomitance that we are able to preserve the sacrificial aspect of the Eucharist.

There is another most enlightening passage of Saint Thomas which I cannot refrain from quoting, in which he emphasizes once more that complete detachment of the Eucharist, considered in its sacramental aspect, from everything that is not Christ's Body and Blood, visualized in their most simple state of reality. In the Third Article of the Eighty-First Question Saint Thomas treats of the communion of the Last Supper when Christ gave to His disciples His Body to eat and His Blood to drink, nay, when He Himself partook of them. The question is whether on that occasion the Body He gave was His impassible, glorious Body. Christ, at that moment, viewed in His natural state, was not in glory. One objector then raises this curious difficulty:

> The words of the sacrament are not now of greater power when they are pronounced by the priest in the person of Christ, than when they were uttered by Christ Himself. But now, through the power of the sacramental words, Christ's impassible and immortal Body is consecrated on the altar. Therefore it was so then, much more truly.

The answer comprises in a few words the whole difference between the power of the sacrament and concomitance.

> The accidents of the Body of Christ are in the sacrament through real concomitance, not through the power of the sacrament: through which there is present the substance of the Body of Christ; and, therefore, the power of the sacramental words goes as far as to be the cause of the Body of Christ being under the sacrament, whatever may be the accidents that are found in it in reality.[130]

This final phrase—*quibuscumque accidentibus realiter in eo existentibus*; whatever may be the accidents that are found in it in reality—is a real stroke of genius. By those accidents of the Body of Christ, Saint Thomas here means His various states, as mortality and glory; they do not enter directly into the nature of the sacrament as such; the sacrament transcends them; the sacrament is equally true, equally potent, equally direct whether Christ be here on earth, as He was at the Last Supper; whether He be dead on the Cross; whether He dwell with His disciples on the shores of the lake after the Resurrection; whether He be ascended to the right hand of the Father in glory. There is no more reason why the Eucharist should have vicissitudes and alterations owing to the varying phases of Christ's wonderful career in His natural state, than, for instance, the sacrament of Baptism should be modified in its innermost constitution according as Christ is either in heaven or on earth.

We do not say, let it be understood, that Christ's natural states are not reflected in the Eucharist; have we not already made it clear, with Saint Thomas, that the Eucharistic Christ would suffer death if the natural Christ were at any time suffering death? The all-important difference is this, that such mirroring of the natural Christ-phases in the Eucharist have nothing to do with the sacrament as such; and, above all, they are to be excluded from the Eucharist in its sacrificial aspect.

As will be seen presently, through real concomitance, neither is the Body without the Blood, nor is the Blood without the Body; but this association is only through real concomitance; it does not interfere with the directness and exclusiveness of the sacramental change of bread into Flesh, and of wine into Blood, in which twofold change there is the whole sacramental representation.

Although the whole Christ be under both kinds [through concomitance], it is so not without purpose. For in the first place this is necessary in order to represent Christ's Passion in

which the Blood was separated from the Body; and, therefore, in the form for the consecration of the Blood mention is
made of its being poured out.[131]

Through concomitance then the whole glorious Christ is in
the Eucharist. This is Catholic faith; Saint Thomas never doubts
it for a moment.

> It is absolutely necessary to confess according to Catholic
> faith that the whole Christ is in this sacrament. We must
> know however that something of Christ is in this sacrament
> in either of the following ways. In one way through the
> power of the sacrament; in another way through natural con-
> comitance.
>
> Through the power of the sacrament there is, under the
> appearances of the sacrament, that into which the pre-existing
> substance of bread and wine is directly changed, as is signi-
> fied through the words of the form, which are effective in
> this as in all other sacraments; as when it is said: *This is my
> Body* or *This is my Blood.*
>
> But through natural concomitance all that is found in the
> sacrament which is joined to that Thing into which the
> aforesaid change terminates. For if two things are joined
> together in reality, then wherever one is in reality, the other
> also must be; it is only through an act of the mind that we
> distinguish those things which are united in reality.[132]

The Council of Trent again employs Thomistic language,
making perfectly clear the difference between sacramental power
and concomitance.[133] It calls this latter "that natural connection and concomitance through which the parts of the Lord
Christ, who is risen already from the dead, who dies no more,
are linked together." As for Christ's Divinity the Council gives
a further reason; it says that Christ's Divinity is present after
the consecration "on account of its admirable Hypostatic

Union with His body and His soul."[134] The Council does not range the Divinity so boldly under concomitance as some other theologians have done.

It would be an interesting point for the historian of Catholic dogma to determine the period when it became convincingly clear to the Church in general that the Eucharist contains the whole Person of Christ. Eucharistic phraseology is almost exclusively what we might call sacramental, all through the centuries; it is only recently that it has become predominantly personal, in the sense of the Eucharist being spoken of as Christ Himself.

Might we not remark that, in our own days, almost the whole of Eucharistic literature, and a vast amount of the Eucharistic worship and devotion, is based more on the concomitant element of the Eucharist than on its sacramental elements? Nothing, of course, could be more legitimate and helpful; we have the whole Christ in the Eucharist; such is Catholic faith.

At the same time we ought not to forget the stern exigencies of Catholic dogma; we must remember that the Eucharist is one of the seven sacraments; above all, that the sacrificial aspect of the Eucharist is saved only through our giving due prominence to what is in the Eucharist *vi sacramenti*. Dogmatically, too, this distinction is supremely vital for the defense of the ancient faith.

The cult of the Eucharist, independently of Mass and Communion, as it is practiced today so much, is certainly justified by all we know from the doctrine of concomitance. But even here, let us remember that, while the whole Christ is in this sacrament—though not in virtue of the sacrament—He is there *per modum sacramenti*; not in a natural mode of being, but in an entirely new mode of being, the sacramental mode. In other words, even the elements of Christ that are in the

Eucharist through concomitance borrow, so to speak, that entirely new mode of existence which Saint Thomas calls a new *esse*, which makes it imperative on us to speak of the Person of Christ in the Eucharist as being the sacramental Christ.

Theologians have exercised all their acumen in finding explanations for the presence of the concomitant elements. We know as a precise dogmatic fact that the Body and Blood of Christ are in the sacrament through Transubstantiation. We do not know, however, how the Soul of Christ is there, as concomitance is not an explanation, like Transubstantiation. Saint Thomas has refrained from any attempt to go beyond the simple meaning of concomitance. There is certainly in the Eucharist a vast undefined region of mystery, which leaves full scope to the mystic, and of which the Catholic mystic has indeed amply availed himself. We have in the Eucharist the clear island of solid rock, its sacramental aspect, with its sacrificial worth; this is simple and direct in concept, clearly defined by the Councils and by tradition. But this island is surrounded by a sea of wonderful mystery, I mean, the vitalities of Christ's infinite Personality.

Some theologians have not been without the courage of their convictions, and have distinguished, in the things belonging to concomitance, between *producibilia et improducibilia*—that is, things that can be produced and things that cannot be produced.[135] Divinity itself cannot be produced; the Soul of Christ, to speak of one thing only, can be produced by the power of God as it is a finite thing. The divine things, then, come into the Eucharist in virtue of divine immensity; the finite things, our bold theologians say, are in the Eucharist through an act of God's power similar to that act which changes bread into Flesh and wine into Blood. It is a direct act of God, but in no wise more marvelous than the act which transubstantiates. The Thing which is the Soul of Christ in heaven is in the Eucharist through the productive act of God as much as the Flesh and the Blood. And so of the other things that constitute Christ.

There is really no reason why the theologian should not exhibit such boldness. God gives us the Flesh and Blood of Christ as it is in reality; it is immaterial after that whether there be the Soul also, with all the qualities of the Soul, but endowed with a sacramental mode of existence. Only let us bear in mind that Christ's Soul in the Eucharist is not there in virtue of the change, but in virtue of an absolute productive act, which absolute act again, no doubt, is only another aspect of some very simple property of the divine omnipotence. Once we admit the fundamental principle that God has power to transpose reality and being from one order into the other, from the natural order into the sacramental order, we have committed ourselves to every possible instance of such transposition.

The aspect of concomitance more directly concerned with the sacrifice of Mass is this, that now the Body is never without the Blood, and the Blood is never without the Body in the Eucharistic sacrifice. For a good many people this dogmatic fact has obscured the fundamental notions of the Eucharistic sacrifice. They seem to be under the impression that, owing to the inseparability of Body and Blood, the Eucharist is not a drastic enough immolation, unless we look elsewhere for sacrificial features. The sacramental Body and Blood do not seem to satisfy their thirst for realities, I might almost say their zeal for ethical achievements.

This is a strange misreading of the Eucharistic mystery, not to say of the very nature of sacrifice. Do we not give to God in the Eucharistic sacrifice the two things He loves best in this world, the Body and Blood of His Son? That such a Body and such Blood be wrapped up in every kind of glory; that they be even enfolded in each other, does certainly not interfere with the perfection of the gift, nor with the precise nature of the gift. There would be no sacrifice if the gift were something less than Body and Blood; but why should the presence of fresh glories in the Body and Blood interfere with the sacrifice? Provided we approach God carrying the Flesh and Blood of the Victim, in virtue of our sacramental ministry, we do a clearly-defined sacerdotal thing. That God should make our gift something fuller than does our ministry, how can this create confusion? In these high regions of divine life realities are inseparable; they accompany each other, without destroying each other's individual identity.

May we not in this connection think of the Incarnation as a greater instance of sacrament and concomitance? Out of three divine Persons, the Second Person only took flesh; yet we know all along that the Word is not without the Father and the Holy Spirit, that the three divine Persons dwell in Christ's Humanity. Yet it is the Son who was born, the Son who lived and died and rose again, not the Father nor the Holy Spirit. In divine things abundance of life is the rule; but in this abundance, distinction of Persons, distinction of missions, remain perfectly clear. In the Eucharist we have not only an abundance of Christ; we have the whole Christ. But in the very midst of that totality the sacrament remains a distinct thing, with a function and a mission all its own.

20

Man's Share in the Eucharistic Sacrifice

At no point in our theological journey do we see to such clear advantage the sacramental concept of the Eucharistic sacrifice as when we arrive at man's role and share in the great mystery.

The Eucharist is essentially a gift to the Church, not only of Christ, but of the sacrifice of Christ; so that the Church herself has her own sacrifice, nay, every Christian has his own sacrifice. To participate in Christ's great sacrifice on the Cross in a merely utilitarian way, by receiving the benefits of such a sacrifice, is only one half of the Christian religion. The full Christian religion is this, that the very sacrifice is put into our hands, so that we, too, have a sacrifice; and we act as men have at all times acted when they walked before God in cleanness of faith and simplicity of heart: we offer to God a sacrifice of sweet odor.

There is a striking sentence in the Sixth Article of the Twenty-Second Question in the Third Part in the *Summa*, which stands out like a signpost at a crossroads. "In the New Law the true sacrifice of Christ is communicated to the faithful under the appearance of bread and wine."[136] It is evident from the context that Saint Thomas here speaks not only of the communication of the graces of Christ's sacrifice, but the sacrifice itself, *verum Christi sacrificium*, is communicated and given to them for their possession and use. The question at issue in that portion of the *Summa* is Christ's Priesthood according to the order of Melchizedek. Is Christ's Priesthood truly according to the order of Melchizedek? Would it not be better to say that Christ's Priesthood is according to the legal rites of the period that followed the mysterious appearance of Melchizedek, when there were the bloody sacrifices of the Temple, as these came much nearer in character to Christ's sacrifice? "In the priesthood of Christ," says Saint Thomas,

> we may consider two things, the offering up (*oblatio*) of Christ, and the participation of that offering. As far as the offering up is concerned, the priesthood of the Law, with its pouring out of blood, was a clearer figure of this priesthood than is the priesthood of Melchizedek, in which no blood is poured out. But when we come to the participation of the sacrifice and to its effect—and it is there that the excellency of Christ's priesthood above the legal priesthood is more evidently apparent—the priesthood of Melchizedek prefigured it much more expressly, because Melchizedek offered bread and wine, which signify, in the words of Saint Augustine, the unity of the Church which is constituted by the participation of the sacrifice of Christ.[137]

The Church is one, says Saint Augustine in so many words, because it has one sacrifice, and that one sacrifice being like the sacrifice of Melchizedek in bread and wine, is truly the sacrifice of Christ handed over bodily to the Church. The Church and her children partake of the fruits of Christ's great sacrifice on the Cross, through the offering up of the same sacrifice. Christ's

Priesthood, according to the order of Melchizedek, is verified in this, that He has given His Church His own sacrifice under the appearance of bread and wine.

This idea, then, of the *participatio sacrificii*, of making over His own sacrifice to the Church, not in results only, but as an act of sacrificial oblation, is what we mean by Christ's great gift to His Church. It is thus we must understand all that is said of the Eucharist as being a participation in Christ's sacrifice: it is the sacrifice itself communicated.

The highest need of man, if we understand man's needs in their true unchangeable nature—that of offering up to God a perfect thing in sacrifice—finds its satisfaction and realization in a sacrament, as all his other needs are provided for by other sacraments. That a sacrament should wash away the dreadful stain of the human race we readily take for granted; that a sacrament should purify our souls from their daily sins, that a sacrament should strengthen and feed us, all this without difficulty becomes part of our thinking.

But let us look higher and think of nobler needs in man's soul. Is there not in us a hunger and thirst for justice; is there not in us the zeal for the glory of God; is there not in us a burning desire to propitiate the divine Majesty for all the sins committed against It? Those cravings, no longer of our weaknesses but of our activities, shall they not be met by a sacrament of equal rank, of the same plane of spiritual outlook? Our active needs have an active sacrament, the sacrament-sacrifice, which is put at our disposal, to be used by us to our heart's content. Would it not endanger the whole of our spiritual estate if in the supernatural life we were only recipients and nothing else; if the sacramental order were nothing but a divine, unceasing enrichment of man, might it not be in danger of sliding away from God, as even heavenly spirits have turned away? But now indeed the center of the sacramental order is something active, tending towards God, for God's own sake: it is the sacrifice unto God of a most sweet odor.

We have, then, for the daily needs of our intercourse with God a sacrifice worthy of Him, the sacrifice offered up by the Son of God Himself. The Eucharistic sacrifice is, therefore, essentially the sacrifice of the Church, for the Church's daily use; and by use we mean, above all things, the worship of God. The Eucharistic sacrifice is not, as was the sacrifice on the Cross, an offering for the whole world; but being a sacramental thing it is for the Church, for every member of the Church, because it is offered up as the sacrifice of the Church, by the children of the Church. "The result which the Passion of Christ brought about in the world, this sacrifice brings about in man.... Hence Our Lord Himself said (Matthew 26): *This is my Blood which will be poured out for you unto the remission of sins.*"[138] We cannot give the Eucharistic sacrifice a scope wider than the Church, because it is the Church only that offers it, and she offers it as her own gift. The sacrifice of the Cross belongs to the whole world, but the Eucharistic sacrifice belongs to the Church only.

It is of supreme importance in this part of theology to avoid passing beyond the limits of the divine institution. Though the Eucharistic sacrifice contains that which made the Calvary sacrifice, it is not a repetition of the universality of that sacrifice. It may truly be said that without the Church the Eucharistic sacrifice would have no meaning, as it would be a sacrifice without a purpose, the whole object of the Eucharistic sacrifice being this, that the Church should have a clean oblation to offer up to God. If the Eucharistic sacrifice is a power in this world that affects even those who are not in the body of the Church, yet it is only through the visible Church that the power is exerted. It cannot be said of the sacrifice of Mass, as it is said of the sacrifice of the Cross, that it redeems mankind; but it redeems the souls of the faithful with an abundance of redemption. The sacrifice of Mass is as much, and as exclusive, a gift to the children of the Church as, say, the sacrament of penance: but instead of its being a direct cleansing of the soul, it is a direct propitiation and glorification of God.

There is no phrase stamped more clearly on the face of Catholic theology than this, that the Eucharistic sacrifice is offered up always and everywhere *in persona Christi*. Christ must be looked upon as the One who offers the Eucharistic sacrifice as truly as He offered the Calvary sacrifice; this is the Catholic faith. In the great Christian sacrifice the Priest and the Victim are one and the same. This identity of Priest and Victim must be preserved at all costs in the Eucharistic sacrifice. Christ is the Priest according to the order of Melchizedek in the sacrifice of bread and wine. As the mortal Christ at the Last Supper offered up for the first time the Eucharistic sacrifice, so does Christ now unceasingly offer up the Eucharistic sacrifice all over the world. Of this we must never lose sight. How, then, are we to reconcile what we have just said about the Church's exclusive privilege of having her own sacrifice with that unceasing and insistent exercise of the sacerdotal function by Christ? If the Victim and the Priest in the Eucharist must be one and the same, how can the Church herself claim to be the sacrificant? Is not this honor entirely appropriated by Christ as much in the Eucharist as it was appropriated by Him on the Cross? Can the Church hope to do more than to assist at the sacrifice, to witness it, to stand in awe before it, to veil her face in adoration?

When Christ gave to the Church that sacrifice in which the Priest and the Victim are always one, He gave her at the same

time a priesthood entirely commensurate with the divine offerings, so that she should have the joys of the priesthood as well
as the benefits of the sacrifice. We have already quoted a text
from Saint Thomas which gives in a few words the solution of
this apparent difficulty. The sacramental sacrifice which we have
from Christ he calls an image of the sacrifice of the Cross. The
priest of the Church in his sacerdotal capacity is the image of
Christ as Priest. In both instances the words have a sacramental
meaning of representation: a sacramental priesthood offers up a
sacramental sacrifice. There is equation between the sacrifice and
the priest; there is the necessary oneness which belongs essentially to the Christian sacrifice.

> As the celebration of this sacrament is a representative image
> of Christ's Passion, so the Altar is representative of the Cross
> itself on which Christ was offered up in His proper species.
>   For the same reason the priest bears the image of Christ,
> in whose person and by whose power he pronounces the
> words of consecration.... And thus in a certain way the priest
> and the victim are one and the same.[139]

This would seem the proper place to speak of the nature of the
Catholic priesthood. Nothing could be more calculated to bring
into a new light the sacramental concept of the Eucharist than a
study of that other sacrament, the Christian priesthood. There
again we find the sacrament at its best and noblest, doing things
in a mode entirely new and *sui generis*. The sacramental character given in the three sacraments of Baptism, Confirmation and
Holy Order belongs to that mysterious sphere of things where
signs become powers. In virtue of the character of Order the
Christian priest bears in himself the image of Christ the Priest,
to the extent of justifying Saint Thomas's saying that there is
identity in the Eucharist between the priest and the victim.

The sacramental character ... is a sign conferring on a man a resemblance to one who is the principal in whom there is full authority for that for which someone else is deputed. Thus soldiers who are sent to the battle are distinguished by the sign of their chief, by which sign they are in a way made like him. And thus those who are deputed to the Christian cult, whose author is Christ, receive a character by which they are configured to Christ. And this is, properly speaking, the character of Christ.[140]

This character, according to Saint Thomas, is in the active powers of the soul, because man is active in his office as priest. For our Doctor sacramental character is the same as *res et sacramentum*.[141] Having, then, a sacramental sacrifice and a sacramental priesthood, the Church is indeed happy in her possessions, and she knows that at no time will her own zeal in offering up sacrifices be a derogation of the all-complete sacrifice of Calvary. On the contrary, is it not her very life endlessly to repeat, out of sheer love, the great role of Christ who is the Priest of God and the Victim of God? Her priesthood is no more an intrusion into Christ's Priesthood than her sacrifice is a supplanting of Christ's sacrifice. In her sacramental genius she knows that her Mass is the living image, the living memory of the holiest thing that ever happened here on earth, the sacrifice of perfect sweetness on Calvary.

The Church considers that every Mass is a new and a complete sacrifice, because at every Mass a priest acts anew, and does what he did not do the day before. The Eucharistic sacrifice is not one continuous act performed by Christ in heaven; it is so many different sacrifices, with a human mode of differentiation. "In many Masses the offering of the sacrifice is multiplied, and therefore the effect of the sacrifice and of the Mass is multiplied."[142]

We must conclude that in the Eucharist Christ is not only the

Victim in a sacramental way, He is also Priest in a sacramental way, not in a natural way as He was Priest on Calvary. He is Priest insofar as He is represented through the character of Order in the celebrant of the Mass; in other words, if there were no sacramental priesthood in the Church there could be no sacramental sacrifice. If Christ such as He is now in His natural state of glory, were directly the sacrificant, there would not be a correspondence between the priest and the victim, as the one would be in the natural state and the other in the sacramental state. But this does not contradict what we said a moment ago that Christ is the High Priest according to the order of Melchizedek, the One who offers up the sacrifice. To offer up the sacrifice through the human priest is essential to a sacramental sacrifice, and it is thus that Christ's great command is carried out: *Hoc facite in meam commemorationem* (Do this in memory of Me).

What He did at the Last Supper His priests do forever, in His Name, in His power, in His Person; as the Council of Trent says—they do what He did. He was the first Priest of the Church, and all other priests are His sacramental images. The priesthood which He exercised at the Last Supper as the Head of the Church goes on in the Church in her own priesthood, which is the sacramental continuation of the priesthood of the Last Supper, as the victim is the sacramental representation of the Calvary sacrifice.

The Catholic Church has a very clear practical working method in this holy thing, her sacrifice. What is the sacrificial worth of each individual Mass offered up? The Church considers that the sacrificial worth of two Masses is just double the sacrificial worth of one Mass; her whole sacramental jurisprudence is based on that principle. This is in perfect conformity with the deepest laws that govern the whole sacramental system given by Christ. Sacraments are not general, universal things; but they are so many sacred acts, each one with a definite spiritual worth. If we let go of the sacramental concept of the Eucharistic sacrifice, I do not see how we could save the individual merit of each Mass, nor how we could defend the Church's jurisprudence in this high matter. But if each Mass is that combination of the human and divine, when the human act of perfect worship contains that mysterious prolongation of the divine immolation, we see how each Mass is a definite event in the history of the world. We are not assisting at one continuous sacrifice, immutably offered up by the Christ in heaven, of which our individual Mass would be merely the transient and local manifestation; but, on the contrary, Mass is offered entirely according to human divisions of time, not always with unbroken regularity. There is one day in the year when there is no celebration; there are more sacrifices on one day than another. Mass is essentially a sacramental action, performed by a sacramental priesthood, not a thing done in heaven, but here on earth, to be counted in human numbers. It is not one unchanging state of Christ; it is the ever-ardent love of the Church offering up her Christ to the Father, intermittently maybe, yet with an ever-increasing devotion. *Hostias et preces Tibi Domine laudis offerimus* (We offer to Thee, O Lord, sacrifices and prayers of praise).[143]

The views expressed in this chapter concerning that perfect communication to the Church by Christ of His sacrifice, of His Priesthood, are very definite Tridentine ideas; I must therefore refer my reader again to the Twenty-Second Session of the Council, of which there is a translation in a former chapter.[144] The language of the Council is so terse that we may read it over and over again before noticing all its implications and all its allusions to Thomistic theology.

Phrases like the following reveal whole spheres of thought

which are truly the heritage of ancient Catholicism. The Eucharistic mystery is instituted by Christ at the Last Supper "in order that He might leave behind for His beloved spouse the Church a visible sacrifice, in keeping with man's nature, by which that bloody sacrifice to be offered up once only on the Cross would be represented."[145]

And again, "Christ instituted the new Pasch, giving Himself to be immolated by the Church through the priests under visible signs, in memory of His passage from this world to the Father."[146]

This great provision of a sacrifice and of a priesthood which Christ made for His Church, had, according to the Council, one great object, namely, "that His Priesthood should not come to an end through death."[147] Christ's Priesthood, then, as well as Christ's sacrifice, is perpetuated directly and fully through the institution of the Catholic priesthood and the Catholic sacrifice. It would be quite a wrong conception of Christ's Priesthood to visualize Him as performing the functions of a priest (specifically and in the full sense of the word) at the right hand of the Father in heaven. If Christ's life in heaven were truly the exercise of priesthood, it would not have been necessary to fear its extinction with His death on the Cross, as the Council supposes. To prevent such extinction, again according to the Council, God gave the sacramental priesthood, with the sacramental sacrifice. Christ's resurrection and glory are not the continuation of the Priesthood; but the sacramental offering and the sacramental priesthood are that continuation on which the Council lays such stress.

The whole sacramental doctrine of Saint Thomas is nothing if not consistent and harmonious. If the sacramental character of the priest enables him to be the sacrificant in Christ's Person, sacramental character also enables the multitude of the faithful to join in that sacrifice in their own way. The sacramental character of Baptism first, and then the sacramental character of Confirmation, are with the sacramental character of Order, though in a lesser degree, figures and resemblances of Christ's Priesthood; and therefore every baptized person is radically fit to communicate in that great sacrifice, to be a sacrificant—at least by participation.

> The sacramental character is a certain participation of the priesthood of Christ in His faithful, in the sense that as Christ has the full power of spiritual priesthood, His faithful also are made like Him in this, that they share in a certain spiritual power with regard to the sacraments and to those things which belong to the divine cult.[148]

Through that specific spiritual thing, the sacramental character, the Christian people are enabled to take a most personal and most direct part in the Eucharistic sacrifice. Their contact with that sacrifice is something more than by faith and devotion; it is a sacramental contact, their character of Christians answering to the sacrificial aspect of the Eucharist in a way which makes of the sacrifice of Mass and the Christian assembly at Mass a truly royal priesthood: "You are a chosen generation, a kingly priesthood, a holy nation, a purchased people: that you may declare His virtues, who hath called you out of darkness into His marvelous light."[149]

I have not attempted in this chapter to treat more fully of the fruits of the sacrifice of Mass in favor of the Church, of the celebrant, of the layman; this part of our theology has been very well expounded by others. I have been concerned chiefly with the human setting of the great sacramental sacrifice, keeping it, as it were, on this earth, though it be not of this earth. I have tried to show how it is the Church's sacrifice, and therefore our sacrifice; how it is a perpetuation of Christ's role, both as Priest and Victim. We succeed as priests to the Christ of the Last Supper; we are not, strictly speaking, the representatives of the Christ in glory when we are at the Altar. The glorious Christ is not represented by any sacrament; as such He is the consummation of the sacraments, not the content of the sacraments, in their true sacramental inwardness.

21

The Eucharistic Liturgy

The Eighty-Third Question of the Third Part of the *Summa* is all about the rite of the sacrament of the Eucharist. The great theologian becomes a keen liturgist. It is remarkable that the very first Article in his lengthy analysis of the liturgical setting of the Eucharist deals with the extremely important question: "Whether Christ be immolated in this sacrament?" As we have already seen, Saint Thomas answers in the affirmative. By subsuming the Eucharistic immolation under the Eucharistic rite, he once more clearly shows how radically sacramentarian is his concept of Mass.

The Eucharistic rite combines sacramental signification in its essential aspect with the extension and enlargement by the Church, under the guidance of the Holy Spirit, of the sacramental formulas of divine origin. When Saint Thomas makes Christ's immolation on the altar part of the Eucharistic rite, he evidently gives to immolation a more active than passive meaning. From his very context he shows that he considers the Church to be the one who immolates Christ on the Altar in the great sacramental action. He does not really attend to the hidden and mysterious things that may happen behind the veil of the Eucharistic appearances, whether Christ be in some unknown form of passive immolation; for him the Church truly immolates Christ as she celebrates the great sacrament, because the sacrament is the literal representation of the Calvary immolation. The Church immolates because she consecrates.

The Eucharistic rite or Liturgy is a fresh confirmation, if such be necessary, of the thesis of this book, that the great Catholic tradition visualizes the Eucharistic sacrifice from the point of view of sacrament. The Church has surrounded the sacrifice of the Eucharist with such splendor, with such rites and ceremonies, as could only befit a treasure entirely her own. Sacraments are the property of the Church, if anything is the property of the Church; and, being her own, she has exploited them with the utmost resourcefulness, adding to the divinely instituted signification, which constitutes the essence of the sacrament, her own signs and symbols, or sacramentals, so as to make of the simple thing given by Christ a glorious celebration, where nature and grace, art and faith, vie with one another in the effort to express the great hidden truth. Now it is my contention that such behavior on the part of the Church is possible only because she considers the sacrifice entrusted to her to be a great sacramental function. She has to perform that function, and she does it with a genius truly divine.

Justin, one of the earliest and most reliable authorities on the Eucharistic rite of the primitive Church, already speaks of that fertility of dramatic inspiration which evidently surrounded the celebration of the Eucharistic mysteries from the very beginning. The celebrant is said by him to offer up Eucharists with great abundance, as much as his strength allows, clearly pointing to a liberty of improvisation which had not been checked by definitive canons of Liturgy.[150]

One remarkable fact of the various Liturgies, both of East and West, is this, that sacrificial language and sacrificial rites are used with great liberty, before and after the essential words of consecration, so that one is often perplexed at first sight to know whether the *oblata*, the things offered, the things sacrificed, are bread and wine or the Body and Blood of Christ; but there is really no puzzle if we remember the profoundly sacramental character of the sacrifice. The Church's total act of offering and oblation is inseparable from the divine contents which at a given moment are brought into her *oblata*. Being an institution composed of men, the Church acts in human fashion, multiplying words and signs in order to bring home a truth too great for adequate expression. In the very midst of the Eucharistic sacrifice she remembers the ancient sacrifices of Abel, Abraham and Melchizedek, and implores God to look upon her own sacrifice with as great favor as He looked on those. Such humility is quite comprehensible if we remember again the sacramental character of the Church's divine sacrifice. It is true that the Holy Thing which she offers is infinitely greater than the offerings of Abel and Abraham and Melchizedek put together; but as she is the sacrificant she craves God's favor, as she might be after all unworthy of presenting so holy a sacrifice.

The sacrifice of Mass is a profoundly human thing, in the sense in which all the sacraments are human things; divine in their innermost kernel, indestructible in their nature, unassailable by man's iniquity, they are still very human in their attendant circumstances; they expand or become narrow, they shine or are obscured, they speak or are silent, according as man, who has their life in his hands, is either generous or niggardly, a child of light or a child of darkness, one who is deaf or one who has his ears open to the things of God. Nowhere else in the realm of creation do we find, things that are so absolutely perfect in themselves, so complete, and so divine, as are the sacraments; which, nevertheless, are left so entirely to man's resources for new fertilities and new perfections. This is the paradox of sacramentalism, and the Eucharist is the most perfect instance of it.

Eucharistic Liturgy, then, may be considered as an expansion by the Church of the sacramental signification. Suppose the Eucharistic sacrifice to be what some are inclined to make it, an entirely divine act, accomplished by Christ, of which the Church is merely the witness, in which she has no active part as sacrificant; then there could be really no Eucharistic Liturgy, in the true sense of the word. There could be hymns and canticles sung around the altar, as we could sing hymns to commemorate the creation of all things; but then we should be merely a circle of worshipers, while the Liturgy is essentially an act, the celebration of a mystery, the expansion of a central sacred rite. We celebrate Mass, let us remember that; we do not only sing at Mass, we make the divine sacrifice, so simple in its essence, dwell amongst us; we detain it amongst us, we are reluctant to see its end, we love to prolong our handling of the divine Victim, till our whole being is thrilled with love and awe. The Church has certainly considered that she has power over the great sacrifice; it being her own possession, she makes it last, she makes it long or short to suit her devotion.

It is sometimes asked: when does Mass—i.e. the essential and technical moment of the sacrifice—really begin? When does it end? The true answer to this ought to be simply that Mass ends when the Church can no longer be considered as a sacrificant. No one word or act of Mass can be pointed out as containing the whole essence of the sacrifice. The thing which Christ did at the Last Supper was not so simple as might appear at first sight. It must have been, on the whole, a prolonged rite, intermingled with the Jewish Pasch, yet easily discernible from it. The Christian Mass, likewise, has never been so simple as certain admirers of primitive forms would like us to believe. Consecration of bread and wine, followed sooner or later by the partaking of the consecrated elements, are essential to Mass; but it would be difficult, not to say impossible, to give intrinsic reasons why the sacrifice is said to be finished, if we had not the very clear rite of the Church, with a beginning and an ending, like all other sacraments. If consecrated wine were reserved in the Tabernacle, as consecrated bread is reserved, this would not mean the continuation of the sacrifice of Mass, as the Church would no longer be the actual sacrificant.

When Our Lord told His Apostles to do this in memory of Him, He evidently ordered them to carry out the rite which they had just seen Him perform, with its thanksgiving, its blessing, its breaking of bread, and the other wonderful circumstances, which must have made such a deep impression on their minds. The institution of this great sacrament is different from the institution of the other sacraments narrated in the Gospels; the Apostles are commanded directly to baptize all nations, they are given power to remit all sins in general terms, without any restrictions. The case is different with the Eucharist; they are told to do what they had just seen with their own eyes. They are not told to consecrate bread and wine, much less are they told to change bread into the Body of Christ or wine into His Blood. The command is of a much sweeter nature: *Hoc facite in meam commemorationem* (Do this in memory of Me). The *hoc* ("this") means all that they had seen and witnessed in the Upper Room. In no other sacrament is rite or liturgy such a constituent element of the sacrament itself: *Et antiquum documentum novo cedat ritui* (Let the old form give way before the new rite).

The sacrifice of Mass, then, being in its very nature a sacramental rite, has always in the history of the Catholic Church had more the appearance of a feast than of a sad memory; we do not make of our daily Mass a Good Friday Liturgy, in which Christ's agony on the Cross is so dramatically brought to our imagination. On the contrary, Mass is all rejoicing; it is the feast of the Church; it is surrounded by every possible splendor; its character—or shall we say its aesthetic aspect?—is borrowed, not from Calvary, but from the spacious Upper Room of the Last Supper, where the Son of God was surely a splendid Host.

The great sacrifice of the Eucharist does not come to us out of an invisible world with the rapidity and the power of lightning; it is not an act of God in the sense in which the creation of light was an act of God; it is human beyond words; it is the feast of love; it is the sacrament of union; it is the banquet which Christ with a great desire wished to eat with His disciples. From the repast of the Supper room the transition to the sacrificial act of the Eucharist was almost insensible. The humanity of it all is simply overpowering; and if it is true that *sacramenta sunt propter homines* (sacraments are for the sake of man), is it not also true that *sacramenta sunt sicut homines* (sacraments are like man)? Sacraments are deeply human. And is there anything more human in the history of the human heart than the celebration of the first Mass when John, the well-beloved, was resting his head on the breast of the divine High Priest?

22

The Eucharistic Banquet

We have come nearly to the end of our book, and perhaps more than one reader may be mildly shocked to find that a book can be written on the Eucharist with so little about Holy Communion. But let me assure my patient friend who has followed me so far that nothing is dearer to me than the Bread of Life. I could write him a whole book on the subject, and not say all I would love to say. But as this little effort bears the name of *A Key to the Doctrine of the Eucharist*, I am not so much a dispenser of the divine Bread as a doorkeeper of the mystical Bethlehem, the House of Bread. The Bread of Life, the Eucharist as the food of man, is not to be found just anywhere and everywhere, but it is essentially a gift from the altar. "The chalice of benediction which we bless, is it not the communion of the blood of Christ? And the bread which we break, is it not the partaking of the body of the Lord?... Behold Israel according to the flesh. Are not they that eat of the sacrifice partakers of the altar?"[151] At no time ought we to forget this great Christian privilege, that we are partakers of the altar of God. It is the glory of the Eucharistic bread that it is not ordinary divine bread, but bread from the altar of God.

There ought not to be in our spiritual attitude to the Eucharist any real separation between Mass and Communion. Suppose, *per impossible*, that there were an extreme multiplicity of private communions by the faithful on the one hand, and an ever-dwindling attendance at the sacrifice of Mass on the other; it would indeed be the gravest spiritual disorder. It would falsify the Eucharistic setting; it would lower the sacrament through a misconception of its true role. The *usus sacramenti*, the use of the sacrament, as Saint Thomas constantly calls it, follows upon the sacrament. The sacrament-sacrifice is followed by the sacrament-food. Such was the order at the institution of the Eucharist, when Christ Himself partook of it, before giving to His Apostles, thus completing in His own Person the whole Eucharistic sacrament.

It is surely a disservice to Catholic truth to describe Holy Communion in terms which many a pantheist might love. The union with God when we eat the Bread of Life affects our spiritual being in a very definite way; it takes us back, as all sacraments do, to the Passion of Christ; we take and eat the holy Thing that is offered up, His Body; we drink the cup of the testament in His Blood. Communion is a sacramental thing, and in this it differs from those other visitations of the Spirit which lead men to God, not sacramentally but personally. Divine things are wonderfully ordered; they do not encroach on each other, their functions are not interchangeable. Not all the work of our spiritual life is done by the sacrament: the Spirit bloweth where He listeth; Eucharistic Communion is not the whole of communion with God; it is a definite communion with the Christ who shed His Blood for us.

The sixth chapter of the Gospel of Saint John, where Christ announces the gift of the Bread of Life, contains no mere promise of a new manna coming down from heaven without passing through the fire of sacrifice. "The bread of God is that which cometh down from heaven and giveth life to the world."[152] Now that Bread of God, Christ Himself, comes down from heaven, not merely as a thing falling gently to the ground to be gathered up by man; it comes down from heaven with the set purpose of being a sacrifice: "Because I came down from heaven not to do my own will, but the will of Him that sent Me."[153] If He is the living Bread, a Bread that will give life to the world, it is because He first has given His Flesh for the life of the world. "This is the bread which cometh down from heaven: that if any man eat of it, he may not die. I am the living bread which came down from heaven. If any man eat of this bread he shall live forever: and the bread that I will give is my flesh, for the life of the world."[154]

These last words, "And the bread that I will give is my flesh, for the life of the world," have a clear sacrificial ring about them. Moreover, that emphatic distinction between flesh and blood, which is such a marked feature of Christ's discourse at Capharnaum, is clearly an allusion to the ever-recurring sacrifices of flesh and blood.

The Eucharistic banquet, then, is essentially a sacrificial banquet: as such it marks a clear separation between light and darkness, between the world and God, between Satan and Christ. "You cannot drink the chalice of the Lord and the chalice of devils: you cannot be partakers of the table of the Lord and the table of the devils."[155] The chalice and table of devils in this text are no mere metaphors, as might appear to some who are always eager to give to the Eucharistic texts of the Scriptures a merely symbolical meaning. Saint Paul means a very material thing, the meats that come from the altar before the idol in the heathen temple. "But the things which the heathens sacrifice, they sacrifice to devils and not to God. And I would not that you should be made partakers with devils."[156]

Let my readers recall the scholastic distinction between "sacrament," "sacrament and thing," and "thing," which I have explained in a former chapter.[157] A favorite idea with Saint Thomas is that the "thing" of the sacrament, or, if you like, the sacramental grace, is the mystical Body of Christ: Christ's sacramental Body makes Christ's mystical Body. The whole Eucharistic spirit is one of charity, a bond between the members of Christ. Here again Saint Paul has the trenchant phrase: "Because there is one bread, we who are many are one body, for we all partake of the one bread."[158] The sacrament signifies this society of the elect, as it signifies the true Body of Christ.

So much is Saint Thomas convinced of this membership with Christ's mystical Body being the essence of the Eucharistic grace in the soul of man that he sees in it the reason why communion in mortal sin is, not only a grievous offense, but actually a sacrilege.

> Whosoever receives this sacrament, signifies by that very fact that he is united to Christ and incorporated in His members. Now this takes place through living faith [i.e. informed by charity] which no one can possess who is guilty of mortal sin. And therefore it is manifest that whosoever receives the sacrament while in mortal sin, commits a falsehood against this sacrament, and accordingly he is guilty of sacrilege, because he violates the sacrament; and for this reason he sins mortally.[159]

Membership with Christ, the whole mystical Body of Christ, ought to be considered the specific Eucharistic grace, as distinguished from all other graces. "He that eateth my flesh and drinketh my blood abideth in Me, and I in him. As the living Father hath sent Me and I live by the Father, so he that eateth Me, the same also shall live by Me."[160] To make this profession of divine membership in a state of mortal sin is a direct violation of truth. Saint Thomas carries that heinous offense to its logical consequences; he calls it *"Falsitas in hoc sacramento,"* a lie in the very midst of the sacrament.

The Eucharistic sacrifice is fundamentally a corporate act, the act of the Church herself; we are never isolated worshipers in the great rite, even when we are but a few gathered around the altar in some remote church, for we are in communion with the whole Catholic Church. So the eating of the divine oblation is always invested with social significance. We all become members of one Body, eating one Bread: this is the classical, traditional concept of the Eucharistic assembly. The society of the elect here on earth are gathered in love and brotherhood, performing such mysterious rites as will open the portals of heaven itself, and invite Angels and men to meet. It would be a disastrous day for the Christian cause if, in the minds of the faithful, the Eucharistic mystery were shorn of that all-important social character, if their frequent eating of the heavenly Bread meant to them nothing more than individual spiritual satisfaction, without promoting the well-being of Christ's mystical Body, the society of the elect.

The world's salvation is in the Eucharist. This is not a hyperbolical phrase; it is a sober statement of spiritual reality. The world's salvation is its entering into the redemptive mystery of Christ. If this mystery becomes the constant preoccupation of human society, its daily deed, its chief concern, its highest aspiration, then society is saved.

Holy Mass makes all the difference between paganism and Christianity; let us be under no illusion about this. There is no charity possible as an institution, as a thing that is a world-power, outside the sacrament of Christ's mystical Body. The ideal world of which the saint dreams is a human society where there is practical knowledge of the meaning of the Eucharistic sacrifice, where men and women have a clear comprehension of the divine mysteries, and where purity and justice are cherished, because without them men would be unfit for the Communion of the Body of God.

23

Eucharistic Consummation

We have seen in one of the earlier chapters that every sacrament has an intimate connection with the future life. Sacraments are true prophecies of the eternal glories. *Et futurae gloriae nobis pignus datur* (And a pledge of future glory is given to us). Saint Thomas calls the sacrament *prognosticum futurae gloriae* (a foretelling of future glory).[161] The sacramental graces, taken in their most specific aspect, have this characteristic of being a pledge of the eternal splendors of the life to come. "In whom (Christ) also believing, you were signed with the Holy Spirit of promise, who is the pledge of our inheritance, unto the redemption of acquisition, unto the praise of His glory."[162] Through the sacraments not only do we receive graces which give us strength to fight the spiritual battle and to conquer eternal life, but in them we are marked and sealed for eternal life. "He that eateth my flesh and drinketh my blood hath everlasting life; and I will raise him up in the last day."[163]

There is, however, in the Catholic sacramental system a certain transitoriness which it is very important to remember. Saint Thomas never tires of alluding to the instrumental character of the sacraments. They are the tools of God to bring about definite results, and when those ends are completely achieved the tools will be laid aside by the divine Artificer. Sacraments belong to the work which Christ does here on earth; they are not permanent glories of the everlasting triumph, "when God shall be all in all." They belong to that definite opus which Christ achieved here below, a task very clearly set Him by the Father, to be done in its own hour. "I have glorified Thee on the earth; I have finished the work which Thou gavest Me to do."[164]

The greatest of the sacraments, the Eucharist, is no exception to this law of transitoriness. The Eucharist, divine as it is, will pass away as faith and hope will pass away; but the graces of the sacrament, the *res sacramenti*, will remain for all eternity, in the perfection of Christ's Mystical Body. The glory for which the Eucharistic mystery prepares us is something greater than the Eucharistic mystery itself. This is admitted by Saint Thomas in the Second Article of the Seventy-Ninth Question. An objector says:

> What is greater cannot be brought about by what is lesser, because nothing acts beyond the limits of its own kind. But it is a lesser thing to receive Christ under a foreign kind, *sub specie aliena*, as happens in this sacrament, than to possess Him in His proper species, *in specie propria*, a thing that belongs to glory. Therefore this sacrament does not cause the acquisition of glory.

In answer Saint Thomas emphasizes the instrumental character of the Eucharist:

> To the third difficulty I say that it is in the very nature of a sacrament that Christ should be taken under a foreign kind, as a sacrament acts instrumentally. But nothing prevents an instrumental cause from producing an effect which is greater than itself.

Divine as the Eucharist is, life with Christ in heaven will be something still more divine. There will be no spiritual waste in the household of God. When the long day of God's work on the souls of men will be ended, He will be found to have given the Bread of Life, the flesh of His Son, with lavish liberality to those who were doing the work of God. But as the work of God was this, to come to Christ in His glory; and as countless multitudes will have come to Christ in His glory, the heavenly Father will be found to have been a generous householder, but not a wasteful one.

The Eucharistic sacrifice shares in the transitoriness of the whole sacramental system; its sacramental character postulates this. There will be no Eucharistic sacrifice in heaven, as there will be no Baptism, no Anointing with Chrism. The Lamb of God will be wedded to His Bride, the Church; the sacrifice of the Lamb will be succeeded by the nuptials of the Lamb.

There has been a tendency with certain pious minds to give to the Eucharistic mystery, and above all to the Eucharistic sacrifice, a heavenly prolongation; not in the sense of all things reaching consummation through the power of the Eucharist, but in the sense of a real continuation of the Eucharistic immolation in its proper kind. Some have spoken of the *sacrificium coeleste* (heavenly sacrifice) as being the third phase of a great sacrificial plan of which the first two phases would be the Calvary sacrifice and the earthly Eucharistic sacrifice. This introduces a useless confusion into theological thought. Heaven has no sacrifice, but is the consummation of all sacrifices. Sacrifice belongs to the period of faith and hope, where things are seen in a dark manner. To introduce sacrificial elements into the clarity of divine vision is to give to the notion of sacrifice an arbitrary extension.

In heaven sacrifices are received, are remembered, are ratified; but they are not celebrated. Heaven sings the glory of the sacrifice as the triumph of the past, as one remembers the day of battle of long ago on which a nation was born to liberty:

> And they sung a new canticle, saying: Thou art worthy, O
> Lord, to take the book and to open the seals thereof: because
> Thou wast slain and hast redeemed us to God, in Thy blood,
> out of every tribe and tongue and people and nation: and
> hast made us to our God a kingdom and priests. And we
> shall reign on the earth.[165]

Whatever we read in the Scriptures of the glories of the
Lamb has reference to the great day when the Lamb was slain
on this earth.

It is clear that Saint Thomas knows of no *sacrificium coeleste*
in the true sense of sacrifice. All sacrificial activity is in the
militant Church. The heavenly Christ is now, even while on
earth there is the daily sacrifice, in a state of consummation,
not in a state of immolation. Now immolation and consummation are contradictory terms in theology; they cannot be
predicated of the same person at the same time, under the
same aspect. The Eucharistic Christ is immolated, the natural
Christ in heaven is consummated; these are two different
aspects of the same Christ; but the heavenly Christ is not at the
same time consummated and immolated. Christ's Priesthood is
eternal, not because the sacrifice is everlasting, but because the
consummation of the sacrifice is eternal. This is the doctrine of
Saint Thomas.

"Does Christ's Priesthood remain for all eternity?" is the title
of the Fifth Article of the Twenty-Second Question in Part
Three of the *Summa*. "How could Christ's Priesthood be eternal," asks an objector, "since the priesthood is necessary to those
only who have the infirmity of sin which may be expiated by
the sacrifice of the priest? But among the saints in heaven there
will be no infirmity of sin." The answer is:

In the office of a priest two things are to be considered; firstly the very offering of the sacrifice, and secondly, the consummation of the sacrifice; which latter is to be found in this, that the end of the sacrifice is reached by those for whom the sacrifice is offered. Now the ends of Christ's sacrifice were not temporal goods, but eternal goods, to which we reach through His death; so it is said in the ninth chapter of Hebrews that Christ is *come an high priest of the good things to come.* For this reason Christ's priesthood is said to be eternal. This consummation of Christ's sacrifice was prefigured by the high priest of the Law entering once a year into the Holy of Holies with the blood of a goat and calf (Leviticus 16); but he did not immolate the goat and the calf in the Holy of Holies, he had immolated them outside; so in like manner Christ entered unto the Holy of Holies, that is to say into heaven itself, and prepared for us the way of entering in there through His blood, which He poured out for us on this earth.[166]

It is clear from this that Saint Thomas, with his firm belief in the eternal Priesthood of Christ, admits of no immolation in heaven. Heaven only knows consummation.

Two more quotations from the same Article will be instructive.

The saints who will be in heaven will not be in need any longer of purification through Christ's priesthood; but having been purified, they will be in need of consummation through that same Christ on whom their glory depends. It is said, therefore, in the twenty-first chapter of Revelation, that *the glory of God enlightens it* (namely the city of the saints), and that *the Lamb is the lamp thereof.*[167]

Although the Passion and Death of Christ are not to be renewed any more, the power of that victim once offered abides forever; as is said in the tenth chapter of Hebrews, that *by one oblation He has consummated forever them that are sanctified.*[168]

Eternity of priesthood in Christ, in the mind of Saint Thomas, is a very definite thing. That glory which was purchased for the elect through the great sacrifice here on earth, natural and sacramental, still depends on the Lamb, who is truly the illuminator of all those who see the Face of God. Christ will show unto the elect that Father whose countenance shines in infinite graciousness because the sweet odor of the ancient sacrifice remains eternally in the remembrance of God.

The altar which figures so prominently in Revelation is not the altar of holocaust, but the altar of incense. In the Exodus the children of Israel receive God's command to fashion articles for the divine worship. The altar of incense and the altar of holocaust are different in style and purpose:

> And all the multitude of the children of Israel being gathered together, He said to them: These are the things which the Lord hath commanded to be done.... The altar of incense and the bars and the oil of unction and the incense of spices: the hanging at the door of the tabernacle: the altar of holocaust, and its grate of brass, with the bars and vessels thereof: the laver and its foot.[169]

In Saint John's vision there is no altar of the holocaust; there only remains the altar of incense.

> And another angel came and stood before the altar, having a golden censer: and there was given to him much incense, that he should offer of the prayers of all the saints, upon the golden altar which is before the throne of God. And the smoke of the incense of the prayers of the saints ascended up before God from the hand of the angel. And the angel took the censer and filled it with the fire of the altar and cast it on the earth: and there were thunders and voices and lightnings and a great earthquake.[170]

The offerings laid on that heavenly altar are no longer Body and Blood, but the prayers of the saints. From the Apocalyptic altar there proceed not mercy and forgiveness, but justice and judgement: "Thunders and voices and lightnings and a great earthquake." It is evidently the altar of consummation, not the altar of propitiation.

Prayer there is in heaven—at least till the great day of the final triumph. Christ in heaven makes unceasing intercession for us. But prayer and sacrifice are not in the same category of spiritual realities, though they both belong to the office of a priest. Saint Thomas teaches that Christ could pray for Himself, but that He could not offer up His sacrifice for Himself.[171] Nothing would be less justifiable than to argue from the continuation of Christ's intercession in heaven to the continuation of Christ's immolation in heaven.

It would be equally impossible to find in the Tridentine presentment of the Christian sacrifice any room for the *sacrificium coeleste*; the Council knows only of the sacrifice accomplished here on earth. The Tridentine Fathers cling to the duality of the bloody sacrifice of Calvary and the unbloody sacrifice of the sacrament; the sacrifice in glory is no part of their theology, in fact, it could not be fitted in with their theology. "If anyone says ... that Christ has not ordered the Apostles and other priests to offer up His Body and His Blood, let him be anathema."[172]

A *sacrificium coeleste* could not be Body and Blood, as Christ in heaven is in fullness of His glory. The sacrifice which Christ, according to Trent, ordered the Church to offer is the sacrifice of His Body and Blood, not the sacrifice of Himself in glory. If there were now a sacrifice truly going on in heaven, our Eucharistic sacrifice here on earth, by the very nature of the supposition, would be merely the earthly representation of that heavenly act. The heavenly act would be continuous, the earthly representations would be successive; but this is not Trent, of course. Body and Blood in the historic sense are the Tridentine notion of sacrifice.

At the end of this book we come back to our point of departure. We started in the simple faith that at Mass we offer up the Body and the Blood of Christ; and to this simple faith we come back now, well persuaded that it is the whole truth. My conclusion then will be an official confession of faith which Gregory XIII exhorts every priest to recite before he approaches the Altar.[173] It is a truly sober Roman summary of the Eucharistic attitude of the Catholic mind.[174]

> I intend to celebrate Mass and to make the Body and the Blood of our Lord Jesus Christ according to the rite of the Holy Roman Church, to the honor of Almighty God and of the whole triumphant Court of heaven, for my benefit and the benefit of the whole militant Church on earth, for all those who have commended themselves to my prayers, both in general and in particular, and for the happy estate of the Holy Roman Church.

Notes

1. "Virtus passionis Christi copulatur nobis per fidem, et sacramenta: differenter tamen; nam continuatio, quae est per fidem, fit per actum animae: continuatio autem, quae est per sacramenta, fit per usum exteriorum rerum." St. Thomas Aquinas, *Summa Theologica*, III, q. 62, a. 6 [hereinafter "*Summa*"].

2. "Sicut antiqui Patres salvati sunt per fidem Christi venturi; ita et nos salvamur per fidem Christi jam nati, et passi." *Summa*, III, q. 61, a. 4.

3. "Membra corporis mystici accipiuntur, non solum secundum quod sunt in actu, sed etiam secundum quod sunt in potentia: quaedam tamen sunt in potentia, quae nunquam reducuntur ad actum; quaedam vero sunt, quae quandoque reducuntur ad actum; et hoc secundum triplicem gradum; quorum primus est per fidem; secundus per charitatem viae; tertius per fruitionem patriae." *Summa*, III, q. 8, a. 3.

4. "Fides est necessaria tanquam principium spiritualis vitae." *Summa*, II-II, q. 16, a. 1, ad 1.

5. *Summa*, II-II, q. 4, a. 4, ad 3.

6. "Sunt autem sacramenta quaedam signa protestantia fidem, qua justificatur homo." *Summa*, III, q. 61, a. 4.

7. Matthew 25:29.

8. "Fides autem unius, immo totius Ecclesiae, parvulo prodest per operationem Spiritus Sancti, qui unit Ecclesiam, et bona unius alteri communicat." *Summa*, III, q. 68, a. 9, ad 2.

9. "Sacramenta sunt necessaria ad humanam salutem triplici ratione." *Summa*, III, q. 61, a. 1.

10. 1 Timothy 3:16.

11. "Nostra autem sacramenta gratiam continent, et causant." *Summa*, III, q. 61, a. 4, ad 2.

12. Ibid., ad 3.

13. "Specialiter autem nunc loquimur de sacramentis, secundum quod important habitudinem signi." *Summa*, III, q. 60, a. 1.

14. "Ad expressiorem significationem gratiae Christi, per quam humanum genus sanctificatur." *Summa*, III, q. 60, a. 5, ad 3.

15. Ibid.

16. *Summa*, III, q. 60, a. 3.

17. 1 Corinthians 11:26.

18. "O sacrum convivium, in quo Christus sumitur; recolitur memoria passionis ejus: mens impletur gratia, et futurae gloriae nobis pignus datur."

19. Romans 6:3-5.

20. Luke 22:19.

21. *Summa*, III, q. 60, a. 4.

22. "Effectus autem intelligibiles non habent rationem signi." Ibid., ad 1.

23. *Summa*, III, q. 60, a. 6, ad 1.

24. "Actus animae, usus exteriorum rerum."

25. *Concilium Tridentinum*, session 7, canon 5.

26. "Sacramenta novae legis simul sunt causae, et signa, et inde est, quod, sicut communiter dicitur, efficiunt quod figurant. Ex quo etiam patet, quod habent perfecte rationem sacramenti, inquantum ordinantur ad aliquid sacrum, non solum per modum signi, sed etiam per modum causae." *Summa*, III, q. 62, a. 1, ad 1.

27. *Summa*, III, q. 62, a. 6.

28. "Nostra autem sacramenta gratiam continent et causant." *Summa*, III, q. 61, a. 4, ad 2.

29. "Causa instrumentalis, si sit manifesta, potest dici signum effectus occulti; eo quod non solum est causa, sed etiam quodammodo effectus, inquantum movetur a principali agente." *Summa*, III, q. 62, a. 1, ad 1.

30. Ephesians 5:26.

31. *Summa*, III, q. 76, a. 7.

32. Ephesians 3:9-10.

33. *Summa*, III, q. 76, a. 7, ad 1.

34. John 3:3-10.

35. *Summa*, III, q. 68, a. 8.

36. *Summa*, III, q. 62, a. 3.

37. Saint Thomas calls it "Virtus quae est fluens, et incompleta in esse naturae." Ibid.

38. *Summa*, III, q. 60, a. 4, ad 2.

39. Ezekiel 1:13-14.

40. *Summa*, III, q. 62, a. 6.

41. "Illud quod nondum est in rerum natura, non movet secundum usum exteriorum rerum." Ibid.

42. *Summa*, III, q. 62, a. 5.

43. Ibid.

44. "Similiter etiam per suam passionem initiavit ritum christianae religionis, offerens seipsum oblationem, et hostiam Deo." Ibid.

45. *Summa*, III, q. 63, a. 6, ad 2.

46. "Illi qui deputantur ad cultum christianum, cujus auctor est Christus characterem accipiunt, quo Christo configurantur." *Summa*, III, q. 63, a. 3, ad 2.

47. *Summa*, III, q. 63, a. 6.

48. *Summa*, III, q. 62, a. 2.

49. "Ratio sacramentalis gratiae se habet ad gratiam communiter dictam, sicut ratio speciei ad genus." Ibid., ad 3.

50. *Summa*, III, q. 69, a. 2, ad 1.

51. "Ac si ipse passus et mortuus esset."

52. "Eucharistia est sacramentum perfectum Dominicae passionis, tanquam continens ipsum Christum passum." *Summa*, III, q. 73, a. 5, ad 2.

53. *Summa*, III, q. 73, a. 4, ad 3.

54. "Ad secundum dicendum, quod id quod est commune omnibus sacramentis, attribuitur antonomastice huic propter ejus excellentiam." Ibid., ad 2.

55. *Summa*, III, q. 73, a. 4.

56. *Concilium Tridentinum*, session 7, canon 1.

57. Ibid., canon 3.

58. "Nam in sacramento Eucharistiae continetur ipse Christus substantialiter; in aliis autem sacramentis continetur quaedam virtus instrumentalis participata a Christo." *Summa*, III, q. 65, a. 3.

59. "Tertio hoc apparet ex ritu sacramentorum: nam fere omnia sacramenta in Eucharistia consummantur, ut Dionysius dicit." Ibid.

60. "Sicut autem se habet virtus Spiritus Sancti ad aquam baptismi, ita se habet corpus Christi verum ad speciem panis, et vini; unde species panis, et vini non efficiunt aliquid, nisi virtute corporis Christi veri." *Summa*, III, q. 73, a. 1, ad 2.

61. "Hoc quod Christus sub aliena specie sumitur, pertinet ad rationem sacramenti, quod instrumentaliter agit. Nihil autem prohibet, causam instrumentalem producere potiorem effectum." *Summa*, III, q. 79, a. 2, ad 3.

62. *Summa*, III, q. 64, a. 5, ad 1.

63. *Summa*, III, q. 73, a. 1, ad 3.

64. "Dicendum quod hoc sacramentum prae aliis habet, quod est sacrificium; et ideo non est similis ratio." *Summa*, III, q. 79, a. 7, ad 1.

65. "Perfectio hujus sacramenti non est in usu fidelium, sed in consecratione materiae." "Repraesentatio Dominicae passionis agitur in ipsa consecratione hujus sacramenti, in qua non debet corpus sine sanguine consecrari." *Summa*, III, q. 80, a. 12, ad 2 and 3.

66. "Quantum ergo ad sacramentum, non minus valet missa sacerdotis mali, quam boni quia utrobique idem conficitur sacramentum." *Summa*, III, q. 82, a. 6.

67. "Hoc sacramentum perficitur in consecratione materiae: usus autem fidelium non est de necessitate sacramenti, sed est aliquid consequens ad sacramentum." *Summa*, III, q. 74, a. 6.

68. "Ad quamdam perfectionem sacramenti pertinet materiae consecratae usus, sicut operatio non est prima, sed secunda perfectio rei." *Summa*, III, q. 78, a. 1, ad 2.

69. "Usus sacramenti est consequenter se habens ad hoc sacramentum." *Summa*, III, q. 82, a. 4, ad 2.

70. "Hoc sacramentum simul est sacrificium, et sacramentum: sed rationem sacrificii habet inquantum offertur; rationem autem sacramenti inquantum sumitur." *Summa*, III, q. 79, a. 5.

71. *Summa*, III, q. 73, a. 6.

72. "Deus, qui nobis sub sacramento mirabili passionis tuae memoriam reliquisti: tribue, quaesumus; ita nos corporis et sanguinis tui sacra mysteria venerari, ut redemptionis tuae fructum in nobis jugiter sentiamus." Commemoration at Lauds during Octave of the Feast of Corpus Christi.

73. John 6:64 (6:63).

74. *Summa*, III, q. 80, a. 2.

75. Ibid., ad 2.

76. "Verba, quibus fit consecratio, sacramentaliter operantur: unde vis conversiva, quae est in formis horum sacramentorum, consequitur significationem." *Summa*, III, q. 78, a. 4, ad 3.

77. *Summa*, III, q. 78, a. 2, ad 2.

78. "Quam oblationem tu, Deus, in omnibus, quaesumus, benedictam, adscriptam, ratam, rationabilem, acceptabilemque facere digneris: ut nobis Corpus et Sanguis fiat dilectissimi Filii tui Domini nostri Jesu Christi."

79. *Summa*, III, q. 81, a. 4, ad 3.

80. Ibid., ad 2.

81. *Summa*, III, q. 81, a. 4.

82. "Et ideo Christus, secundum quod est sub hoc sacramento, pati non potest, potest tamen mori." Ibid., ad 1.

83. The distinction between "sacrament" and "sacrament and thing" is discussed in chapter 8.

84. St. Augustine, *On the Creed* (*De Symbolo*), book III, chapter 7.

85. "In illo triduo mortis Christi dicendum est, quod totus Christus fuit in sepulchro: quia tota persona fuit ibi per corpus sibi unitum: et similiter totus fuit in inferno: quia tota persona Christi fuit ibi ratione animae sibi unitae: totus etiam Christus tunc erat ubique ratione divinae naturae." *Summa*, III, q. 52, a. 3.

86. Ibid., ad 1 and 2.

87. 1 Corinthians 11:26.

88. "Haec autem est differentia inter Eucharistiam et alia sacramenta habentia materiam sensibilem, quod Eucharistia continet aliquid sacrum absolute, scilicet ipsum Christum." *Summa*, III, q. 73, a. 1, ad 3.

89. "Eucharistia est sacramentum passionis Christi, prout homo perficitur in unione ad Christum passum." *Summa*, III, q. 73, a. 3, ad 3.

90. "Sicut enim quod ubique offertur, unum est corpus, et non multa corpora, ita et unum sacrificium." *Summa*, III, q. 83, a. 1, ad 1.

91. "Etiam ante passionem Christi baptismus habebat efficaciam a Christi passione, inquantum eam praefigurabat: aliter tamen, quam sacramenta veteris legis, nam illa erant figurae tantum; baptismus autem ab ipso Christo virtutem habebat justificandi, per cujus virtutem ipsa etiam passio salutifera fuit." *Summa*, III, q. 66, a. 2, ad 1.

92. *Summa*, III, q. 83, a. 1. The internal citation is to Revelation 13:8.

93. *Summa*, III, q. 62, a. 6.

94. The Latin of Saint Thomas which expresses this could not be more terse: "Celebratio autem hujus sacramenti imago quaedam est repraesentativa passionis Christi, quae est vera ejus immolatio; et ideo celebratio hujus sacramenti dicitur Christi immolatio." *Summa*, III, q. 83, a. 1.

95. Psalm 109:4 (110:4).

96. Luke 22:19; 1 Corinthians 11:24.

97. Colossians 1:13.

98. Hebrews 4:16.

99. *Concilium Tridentinum*, session 22, chapters 1, 2.

100. *Summa*, III, q. 22, a. 3, ad 2.

101. Exodus 29:25.

102. Genesis 8:20-21.

103. Ephesians 5:2.

104. *Summa*, III, q. 48, a. 3, ad 1.

105. "Passio Christi, secundum quod comparatur ad divinitatem ejus, agit per modum efficientiae: inquantum vero comparatur ad voluntatem animae Christi, agit per modum meriti: secundum vero quod consideratur in ipsa carne Christi, agit per modum satisfactionis, inquantum per eam liberamur a reatu poenae; per modum vero redemptionis, inquantum per eam liberamur a servitute culpae; per modum autem sacrificii, inquantum per eam reconciliamur Deo." *Summa*, III, q. 48, a. 6, ad 3.

106. Philippians 2:8-9.

107. "Christus autem consecutus est per suam passionem gloriam resurrectionis, non quasi ex vi sacrificii, quod offertur per modum satisfactionis, sed ex ipsa devotione, qua secundum charitatem humiliter passionem sustinuit." *Summa*, III, q. 22, a. 4, ad 2.

108. *Summa*, III, q. 49, a. 4. The internal citation is to 1 Kings 26:19 (1 Samuel 26:19).

109. John 10:17-18.

110. Hebrews 9:11-15.

111. Hebrews 9:25-28.

112. See text accompanying note 76, at p. 65.

113. "Deus conjugavit divinitatem suam, idest divinam virtutem, pani et vino, non ut remaneant in hoc sacramento, sed ut faciat inde corpus et sanguinem suum." *Summa*, III, q. 75, a. 2, ad 1.

114. "Corpus Christi non est eo modo in hoc sacramento, sicut corpus in loco, quod suis dimensionibus loco commensuratur, sed quodam speciali modo, qui est proprius huic sacramento: unde dicimus, quod corpus Christi est in diversis altaribus, non sicut in diversis locis, sed sicut in sacramento: per quod non intelligimus, quod Christus sit ibi solum sicut in signo, licet sacramentum sit in genere signi; sed intelligimus corpus Christi hic esse secundum modum proprium huic sacramento." *Summa*, III, q. 75, a. 1, ad 3.

115. "Sicut autem se habet virtus Spiritus Sancti ad aquam baptismi, ita se habet corpus Christi verum ad speciem panis et vini." *Summa*, III, q. 73, a. 1, ad 3.

116. *Summa*, III, q. 75, a. 4, ad 3.

117. "Corpus Christi remanet in hoc sacramento, non solum in crastino, sed etiam in futuro, quousque species sacramentales manent, quibus cessantibus, desinit esse corpus Christi sub eis, non quia ab eis dependeat, sed quia tollitur habitudo corporis Christi ad illas species: per quem modum Deus desinit esse dominus creaturae desinentis." *Summa*, III, q. 76, a. 6, ad 3.

118. *Summa*, III, q. 75, a. 1.

119. Ibid.

120. *Summa*, III, q. 75, a. 8, ad 3.

121. "Non enim haec conversio fit per potentiam passivam creaturae, sed per solam potentiam activam creatoris." Ibid., ad 4.

122. *Summa*, III, q. 78, a. 1.

123. Luke 18:24-27.

124. "Christo autem non est idem esse secundum se, et esse sub hoc sacramento; quia per hoc quod dicimus ipsum sub hoc sacramento, significatur quaedam habitudo ejus ad hoc sacramentum." *Summa*, III, q. 76, a. 6.

125. *Salmanticenses*, tome 18, p. 304. [Note: The Salmanticenses, Discalced Carmelite theologians of Salamanca, Spain (16th-17th centuries), were especially conscientious followers of Thomas Aquinas, whose work has "ever been held in the highest esteem, particularly at Rome." *The Catholic Encyclopedia*, vol. XIII, p. 402 (1912).]

126. "Suavi tractatu discurrere secundum potentiam sacramentorum eorumque ordinem." Tommaso de Vio Cardinal Cajetan, *Commentary on the Summa Theologica of St. Thomas Aquinas*, q. 75, a. 1, com. 11.

127. *Summa*, III, q. 80, a. 5.

128. Ibid., ad 1.

129. "Convertitur forma panis in formam corporis Christi, secundum quod dat esse corporeum, non autem secundum quod dat esse animatum tali anima." *Summa*, III, q. 75, a. 6, ad 2.

130. "Accidentia corporis Christi sunt in sacramento ex reali concomitantia, non autem ex vi sacramenti, ex qua est ibi sub-

stantia corporis Christi; et ideo virtus verborum sacramentalium ad hoc se extendit, ut sit sub sacramento corpus Christi, scilicet quibuscumque accidentibus realiter in eo existentibus." *Summa*, III, q. 81, a. 3, ad 3.

131. *Summa*, III, q. 76, a. 2, ad 1.

132. *Summa*, III, q. 76, a. 1.

133. See *Concilium Tridentinum*, session 13, chapter 3.

134. "Divinitatem porro propter admirabilem illam ejus cum corpore et anima hypostaticam unionem."

135. See, e.g., *Salmanticenses*, tome 18, p. 64; see also note 125.

136. "In nova lege verum Christi sacrificium communicatur fidelibus sub specie panis, et vini."

137. *Summa*, III, q. 22, a. 6, ad 2.

138. *Summa*, III, q. 79, a. 1. The internal citation is to Matthew 26:28.

139. *Summa*, III, q. 83, a. 1, ad 2 and 3.

140. *Summa*, III, q. 63, a. 3, ad 2.

141. See chapter 8 for an explanation of *"res et sacramentum."*

142. "In pluribus vero missis multiplicatur sacrificii oblatio: et ideo multiplicatur effectus sacrificii, et sacramenti." *Summa*, III, q. 79, a. 7, ad 3.

143. Offertorium in Requiem Mass.

144. See text accompanying notes 95 to 99, pp. 100-101.

145. "Ut dilectae sponsae suae Ecclesiae visibile, sicut hominum natura exigit, relinqueret sacrificium, quo cruentum illud, semel in cruce peragendum, repraesentaretur." *Concilium Tridentinum*, session 22, chapter 1.

146. "Novum instituit Pascha, seipsum ab Ecclesia per sacerdotes sub signis visibilibus immolandum in memoriam transitus sui ex hoc mundo ad Patrem." Ibid.

147. "Quia tamen per mortem sacerdotium ejus extinguendum non erat." Ibid.

148. *Summa*, III, q. 63, a. 5.

149. 1 Peter 2:9.

150. St. Justin Martyr, *The First Apology*, chapters 65 and 67.

151. 1 Corinthians 10:16, 18.
152. John 6:33.
153. John 6:38.
154. John 6:50-52.
155. 1 Corinthians 10:21.
156. 1 Corinthians 10:20.
157. See chapter 8.
158. 1 Corinthians 10:17.
159. *Summa*, III, q. 80, a. 4.
160. "Qui manducat meam carnem et bibit meum sanguinem, in me manet, et ego in illo. Sicut misit me vivens Pater, et ego vivo propter Patrem: et qui manducat me, et ipse vivet propter me." John 6:56-57.
161. *Summa*, III, q. 60, a. 3.
162. Ephesians 1:13-14.
163. John 6:54.
164. John 17:4.
165. Revelation 5:9-10.
166. *Summa*, III, q. 22, a. 5. The internal citation is to Hebrews 9:11.
167. *Summa*, III, q. 22, a. 5, ad 1. The internal citation is to Revelation 21:23.
168. *Summa*, III, q. 22, a. 5, ad 2. The internal citation is to Hebrews 10:14.
169. Exodus 35:1, 15-16.
170. Revelation 8:3-5.
171. *Summa*, III, q. 21, a. 4, and q. 22, a. 4.
172. *Concilium Tridentinum*, session 22, canon 2.
173. Pope Gregory XIII (1572-1585).
174. "Ego volo celebrare Missam, et conficere Corpus et sanguinem Domini nostri Jesu Christi, juxta ritum sanctae Romanae Ecclesiae, ad laudem omnipotentis Dei, totiusque Curiae triumphantis, ad utilitatem meam totiusque Curiae militantis, pro omnibus qui se commendaverunt orationibus meis in genere et in specie, et pro felici statu sanctae Romanae Ecclesiae."

Index

L

PETER KREEFT is a professor of philosophy at Boston College. He is a regular contributor to several Christian publications, and is the author of over forty books, including *Three Philosophies of Life*, *Prayer: The Great Conversation*, and *Fundamentals of the Faith*.

AIDAN NICHOLS, O.P., is a priest of the Dominican Order who has taught at the Pontifical University of St. Thomas, Rome, and Blackfriars Hall, Oxford. He has written some thirty books, including *Discovering Aquinas: An Introduction to His Life, Work, and Influence*. Father Nichols is Prior of the Dominican Priory of St. Michael, Cambridge.

A NOTE ON THE TYPE

The text of this book is set in a digitized version of Garamond. Named for the French Renaissance printer Claude Garamond, this typeface has been a favorite of book designers for four centuries.

Legible in the highest degree, yet not monotonous in color, Garamond is a quietly elegant type that can be read for hours without wearying the eye.

Zaccheus Press

Zaccheus Press is a small Catholic press devoted to publishing fine books for all readers seeking a deeper understanding of the Catholic faith.

To learn more about Zaccheus Press, please visit our webpage. We welcome your comments, questions, and suggestions.

www.zaccheuspress.com

And behold, there was a rich man named Zaccheus, who was the chief among the tax collectors. And he sought to see Jesus, but could not because of the crowd, for he was short of stature. So he ran ahead and climbed up into a sycamore tree to see Him, for He was going to pass that way.

—Luke 19:2-4